Linnea and Alex
Happy 7th Anniversary

There was a particular argument
regarding this. Martin's choice. I
thought a recipe book would be
better, however, for once Martin
the argument! Enjoy. It look
lovely book.   Love
                        Mom and Martin

7th is wood & cop...

THE SELKIRKS
NELSON'S MOUNTAINS

THE SELKIRKS
NELSON'S MOUNTAINS

by J.F. Garden

Introduction by
William Lowell Putnam

Photographs by   F. Duchman
                  G. Boles
                  J.F. Garden
                  R. Laurilla
                  J. Maitre
                  M. Pirnke
                  U. Veideman

Design and layout by Catherine Garden
Editor, Penny Graham
Typist, Shirley Magus

Printed and bound by Dai Nippon, Japan
Typesetting by United Graphic Services Ltd.

ISBN 09691621-0-3

Copyright J.F. Garden 1984
Footprint Publishing
Box 1830
Revelstoke, BC   V0E 2S0

front cover photo
Moby Dick (10460')   *R. W. Laurilla*

back cover photo
Alpine flowers   *R. W. Laurilla*

page 1
Evergreen Buds   *J. F. Garden*

pages 2 and 3
The Selkirks   *R. W. Laurilla*

4

THE PHOTOGRAPHERS

GLEN BOLES is a long time resident of Calgary, Alberta and is a veteran mountain climber and skier. His love of the mountains is obvious in his photographs and in his pen and ink reproductions of the peaks he has known.

FRED DUCHMAN resides in Revelstoke, BC and is a man of many talents. Mountaineer, skier, photographer, carpenter, he is accomplished at all he does. He and his family reside in a picturesque house which he himself built.

ROGER LAURILLA is an aspiring mountain guide and talented photographer. He is a native of the Selkirks, having grown up at Flat Creek, BC and now works for Canadian Mountain Holidays in the winter. What does he do in the summer? Climb!

JIM MAITRE is a native of Ontario who, upon venturing west, fell in love with the mountains. He has climbed in the Rockies, Selkirks, Southern Alps of New Zealand and the Cordillera Blanca of Peru. The mountains have captured his spirit!

MIKE PIRNKE, also a resident of Revelstoke, BC, is a surveyor by trade, but his nature photographs are such that one wonders why he is not a well known and famous photographer.

DUSTY VEIDEMAN is an old pro in the field of photography. He owns the "Photo House" in Revelstoke, BC where one can purchase framed enlargements of his beautiful photographs of the Selkirk and Monashee Mountains. He is also a very experienced pilot and mountain flyer. C-FHCJ, his Piper Super Cub is a remarkable photo aircraft and most trustworthy amongst the Selkirk peaks.

Bald Eagle (Haliaeetus leucocephalus)
M. Pirnke

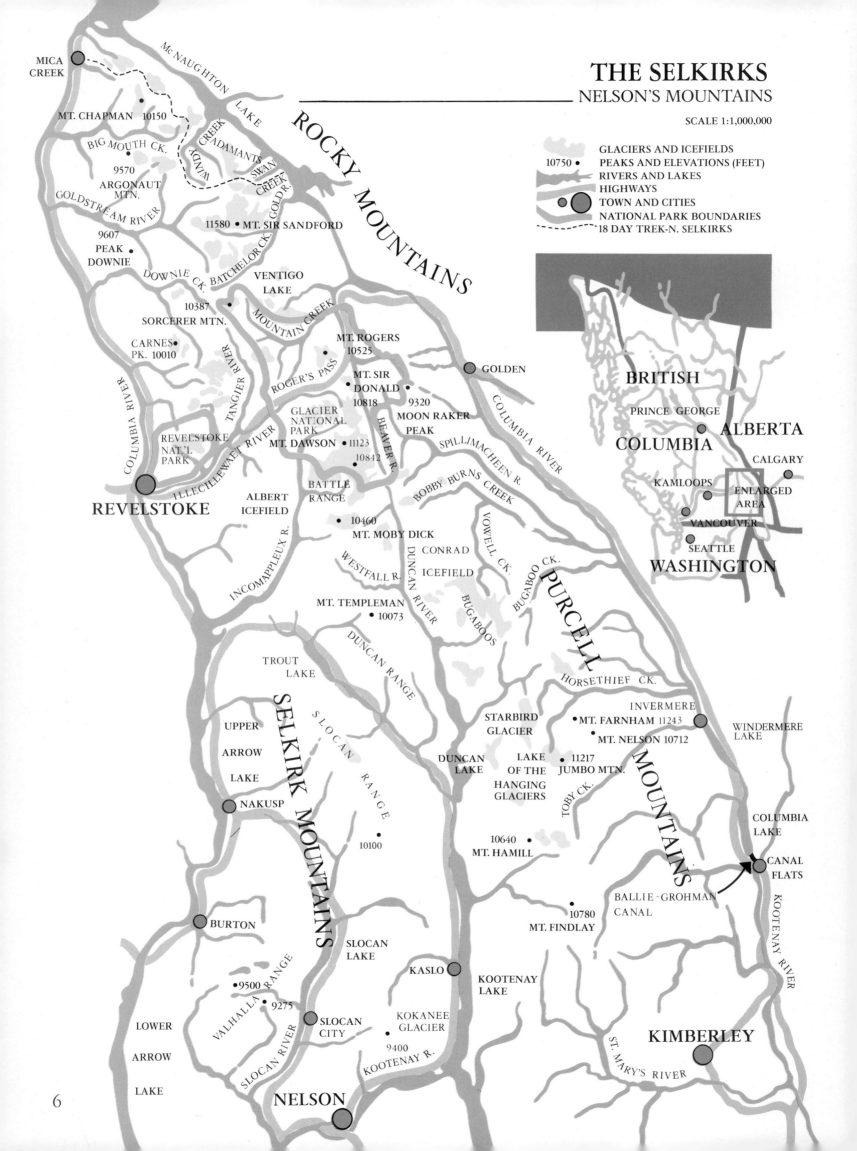

THE SELKIRKS
NELSON'S MOUNTAINS

SCALE 1:1,000,000

GLACIERS AND ICEFIELDS
10750 • PEAKS AND ELEVATIONS (FEET)
RIVERS AND LAKES
HIGHWAYS
TOWN AND CITIES
NATIONAL PARK BOUNDARIES
18 DAY TREK-N. SELKIRKS

MICA CREEK

McNAUGHTON LAKE CREEK

MT. CHAPMAN 10150

BIG MOUTH CK.

GRADAMANTS

WINDY CREEK

SWAN CREEK

GOLD R.

ROCKY MOUNTAINS

9570

ARGONAUT MTN.

GOLDSTREAM RIVER

9607 PEAK DOWNIE

11580 • MT. SIR SANDFORD

DOWNIE CK. BATCHELOR CK.

VENTIGO LAKE

10387 SORCERER MTN.

MOUNTAIN CREEK

CARNES PK. 10010

TANGIER RIVER

ROGER'S PASS

MT. ROGERS 10525

GOLDEN

COLUMBIA RIVER

MT. SIR DONALD 10818

9320 MOON RAKER PEAK

COLUMBIA RIVER

GLACIER NATIONAL PARK

BEAVER R.

SPILLIMACHEEN R.

REVELSTOKE NAT'L PARK

MT. DAWSON • 11123
10842

ILLECILLEWAET RIVER

REVELSTOKE

ALBERT ICEFIELD

BATTLE RANGE

BOBBY BURNS CREEK

VOWELL CK.

BUGABOO CK.

PURCELL

INCOMAPPLEUX R.

• 10460
MT. MOBY DICK

WESTFALL R.

CONRAD ICEFIELD

DUNCAN RIVER

BUGABOOS

MT. TEMPLEMAN • 10073

DUNCAN RANGE

TROUT LAKE

HORSETHIEF CK.

INVERMERE

STARBIRD GLACIER

MT. FARNHAM 11243

WINDERMERE LAKE

UPPER ARROW LAKE

SLOCAN RANGE

DUNCAN LAKE

LAKE OF THE HANGING GLACIERS

MT. NELSON 10712

11217 JUMBO MTN.

TOBY CK.

MOUNTAINS

COLUMBIA LAKE

NAKUSP

10100

10640 •
MT. HAMILL

COLUMBIA LAKE

CANAL FLATS

BALLIE - GROHMAN CANAL

KOOTENAY RIVER

SELKIRK MOUNTAINS

BURTON

SLOCAN LAKE

10780 •
MT. FINDLAY

VALHALLA RANGE

• 9500

• 9275

SLOCAN CITY

KASLO

KOOTENAY LAKE

KOKANEE GLACIER

KIMBERLEY

LOWER ARROW LAKE

SLOCAN RIVER

9400

KOOTENAY R.

ST. MARY'S RIVER

NELSON

(Inset map)
BRITISH COLUMBIA

PRINCE GEORGE

ALBERTA

KAMLOOPS

CALGARY

ENLARGED AREA

VANCOUVER

SEATTLE

WASHINGTON

6

TABLE OF CONTENTS

FOREWORD

When I was 16, I began climbing. Previously, I had been exposed to the mountains on weekend fishing trips with my father. I have been influenced by mountain surroundings for some 25 years and during the past seven, have lived and breathed the Selkirks.

I do not consider myself as much a mountain climber as an alpinist. I am not a high-angle face climber, though I do enjoy the challenge of attaining the high peaks. As an alpinist, I am interested in all aspects of our alpine world from skiing to hiking and climbing, to flora and fauna and also in the geology which has formed that world.

As I became involved in mountain activities, many including family and friends, have expressed their fears of venturing into what they consider to be an entirely hostile and dangerous environment. Their world has remained largely urban and man-made, virtually void of the multifaceted world of nature. Therefore, in "The Selkirks - Nelson's Mountains" I wish to present a photographic and written account of the natural environment, allowing others the opportunity to enjoy and experience some of the alpine world that I and fellow companions have come to know. I wish to present the human dimension of the alpine experience, a dimension not often included in photographic books of this design.

My basic aim is to illustrate the mood and spirit of the mountains. There is drama and struggle involved in the exploration and conquest of these high peaks but also serenity and beauty in the many hidden utopias existing in the mountain valleys. I hope to unfold for the reader an understanding of the heritage of the Selkirks, their natural and cultural history.

This book is not just for the climber, as I do not consider myself just a climber. Nor do I consider the mountains as the exclusive domain of the climber. Rather this project is for all those who may hold any appreciation for the spectacular natural world which we are so fortunate to have and behold at our doorstep. Perhaps through this book, a better understanding, a better awareness and thus a more assured future will exist for one of our last remaining strongholds of nature.

To those people who have assisted in and encouraged the concept of "The Selkirks - Nelson's Mountains", I owe unending thanks and appreciation. Many individuals have influenced this venture in one way or another. First and foremost are my fellow photographers Fred Duchman, Glen Boles, Roger Laurilla, Jim Maitre, Mike Pirnke and 'Dusty' Veideman. The greatest contribution that has made this book possible, came from three ladies who proved themselves indispensable. Cathy Garden, who is a commercial artist, designed and organized the book with exceptional artistic flair. Penny Graham, as editor, provided the guidance and patience necessary to develop a polished manuscript. Shirley Magus had the magic ability of translating written manuscript and scribblings to typewritten text. Lastly I have to thank all my friends and family for their encouragement and the people of Revelstoke who were as anxious as I to see the end result.

John F. Garden
Revelstoke, BC
May 14, 1984

facing page

Western Anemone (Anemone occidentalis)
J. F. Garden

INTRODUCTION

This is the book I once set out to write. It deals with the adventures and challenges, joys and tribulations of God's wilderness. The Selkirks are the most historic of Canadian mountains and though so close to paths of modern transportation, still (absent the use of helicopters) the most difficult of access.

Here is recounted with love and wonderment the tale of a budding alpinist as he, like many generations before him, came to know the risks and rewards of alpinism. These are the mountains once named for Horatio, Lord Nelson, a celebrated hero of the British nation. But for well over a century they have carried the name of Thomas Douglas, the Fifth Earl of Selkirk, and one of the great figures of Canadian history.

Though it is perennially fashionable for the elders in any field of human endeavor to look back at what they term the "good, old days" and to point out how much easier things are now for those following along (yet all these points are relative for though certain trails may be easier, certain maps more accurate, certain equipment more suitable) the human spirit provides a stimulus to seek ever more difficult goals. The balance is maintained in accomplishment.

When I first visited these ranges there were none of the accurate large-scale maps made possible in recent years by wide-spread aerial photography. Indeed, such maps as were available, could be trusted only to show accurately the locations of peaks that could be triangulated from high points near the railway survey belt. Only certain of major streams (where prospectors had struck pay-dirt) had their courses reliably shown. In those days,

one could spend a two week period floundering hopelessly in search of access to an attractive summit, only to find at the end when one's vacation was over, that next summer we'd have to try a different valley.

With modern maps and aerial support the days of interminable bushwhacking are no longer required and those who do not feel the urge to penance can pay to avoid this unpleasantness. But as certain tasks and some of the risks associated with exploration and mountaineering have become more controllable and eased by the advances of our civilization, the human spirit, as this story indicates raises its expectations accordingly.

And the loving eye of a thoughtful climber always seeks out and respects the delicate and fleeting beauties of the natural order that can only be found far removed from the hand and works of man. They become ever more precious as with each passing day they become ever more rare.

William Lowell Putnam

facing page
Mountain Stream   *R. W. Laurilla*

Goat's Fodder - Lichen   J. F. Garden

facing page
Indian Paintbrush in the Rocks
(Castilleja miniata) J. F. Garden

NELSON'S MOUNTAINS

THE SELKIRKS - NELSON'S MOUNTAINS

An island has long been defined as a mass of land surrounded by water. If such a definition stands in all instances, then there exists, within the southeastern cordillera of the province of British Columbia, an island.

This island is a spectacularly mountainous area, almost totally uninhabited by man and completely surrounded by water in the form of two rivers and a man-made canal. The two rivers are the mighty Columbia and its tributary, the Kootenay. The canal is the Baillie-Grohmann Canal connecting the two rivers over a low marshy divide at Canal Flats, British Columbia. Here exists an island of mountains some 300 miles in length bounded by the Columbia River in its great bend to the north and by the Kootenay River in its long swing southward through Idaho and Montana, and northward again joining the Columbia at Castlegar, BC.

Contained within this mountainous island bounded by the Columbia River system are a series of ranges which compose the Selkirks, rivalling anywhere on earth for beauty and impressive ruggedness. Civilization barely encroaches upon the margins of this island. Access is limited to the adventurous and most hardy.

page 14
Winter Sunset - Mt. Revelstoke
National Park
U. Veideman

The first white man to record the sight of the Selkirk Mountains seems to have been totally awestruck by their presence. He named them Nelson's Mountains following the most important event of his generation, the Battle of Trafalgar and the heroic death of Horatio Nelson.

That individual was David Thompson, geographer and astronomer to the North-West fur trading company. In 1807 he stood on the banks of the Columbia River and upon viewing a magnificent mountain to the west of what is now Invermere, British Columbia, bestowed Lord Nelson's name on it and the surrounding mountain range. It is unknown who later applied the name Selkirks to Nelson's Mountains but when the North-West and Hudson's Bay fur trading companies merged in 1821, it became common to refer to the range as the Selkirk Mountains in honour of Thomas Douglas, Fifth Earl of Selkirk. He was one of the major promoters of the Hudson's Bay Company and a significant figure in the evolution of Canada.

With continued exploration, the Selkirks became further defined geographically, especially during the Palliser Expedition of 1857-1860. Dr. James Hector then applied the name Purcell to the eastern range between the Beaver-Duncan divide and Rocky Mountain Trench. The name honoured Dr. Goodwin Purcell of Trinity College, England, a member of the expedition's selection committee.[1]

The Purcells and Selkirks and associated ranges which compose these mountains are of such homogeneous origin and composition, consideration of one must certainly involve the other. David Thompson was, therefore, quite correct by naming all the mountains he viewed to the west of the Columbia River at Invermere as Nelson's Mountains.

Settlement and land development along the margin of the Selkirk Mountains in the 1880's led to construction of the canal which has created the island. W.A. Baillie-Grohman appeared in the Kootenay district in 1883 and upon discovering the proximity of the Kootenay River to Columbia Lake (the headwater of the Columbia River) he schemed to construct a canal to allow diversion of water from the Kootenay to the Columbia in order to facilitate draining of his marsh land at the head of Kootenay Lake. The Kootenay passes within a mile of the Columbia Lake with little or no difference in elevation separating the two and had been known to overflow into the Columbia system.

Baillie-Grohman's ambitions were thwarted however, when his canal project became a white elephant following government intervention on behalf of downstream plaintiffs on the Columbia River. The Canadian Pacific Railway was afraid of flood damage to its bridges below Golden and Revelstoke. Eventually the Baillie-Grohman Canal became a part of the history of the region and the final link in the creation of the island of mountains.

The Selkirk Mountains stand largely untouched by the hand of man and remain much as they have since their natural evolution began hundreds of millions of years ago. They have survived continuous deformation by natural processes and the unthinking onslaught of man. They remain a monument to nature and the incredible forces which are nature.

Much speculation backed by a smattering of physical evidence, has allowed us to envision what natural processes occurred in ancient geologic times. It is fairly easy to speculate on the ice-age era as evidence remains largely undisturbed. Past eons of mountain building and deformation are however much harder to determine and therefore the true sequence of events can never be fully known. Geologists can, through detailed study of facts, come up with general theories and despite much controversy and disagreement, provide us with a good idea what produced the mountain landscapes.

The geologic history of the Selkirks is complex. They are composed of some of the oldest sedimentary rocks found within the western cordillera of Canada. The Selkirks had their beginnings some 600 million years ago in a shallow ocean shelf off-shore of what would have been a totally unrecognizable North American continent. As sediments poured in off the land mass, subsidence of the coastal shelf created tremendously thick accumulation. Interruptions in the form of crustal deformation often took place. Uplift and subsequent erosion occurred, indicated now by the absence of certain rock layers that should otherwise be seen in the record of the rocks.

Drastic alterations of sedimentary rock through heat, chemical reaction, and mechanical force led to the formations of metamorphic rock and the great contortions and patterns we see along the mountain walls. Prior to the evolution of the Rocky Mountains to the east, the Selkirks finally stood unsurpassed in height, dominating the western margin of the continent of North America. The range was probably separated from the continent proper by shallow seas into which sediments were pouring as the Selkirk's were down-wasted by the elements. Even in ancient times, the land which the Selkirks dominated was likely an island!

As sediments were deposited, subsiding into the shallow sea between the Selkirk Mountains and the continent, massive influxes of molten rock periodically coursed through the Selkirk's deep roots causing further uplift. With the pressures of continental drift causing an eastward migration of the ranges, the earth's crust was forced downward below the massive accumulations of the Rocky Mountain sedimentary basin.

Fireweed (Epilobium augustifolium)
R. W. Laurilla

18

Great fractures and breaks in the crust allowed molten rock to flow freely upward into the Selkirk Ranges, cooling gradually over millions of years into crystalline granitic rocks. As a result of these continuous pressures there was a long period of complex folding, faulting and displacement along the Rocky Mountain Trench. This produced destruction and deformation the likes of which man cannot possibly comprehend. That episode, begun perhaps 100 million years ago, resulted in a shortening of the earth's crust by as much as 100 miles and a thickening of some five miles. The Rocky Mountains as we now know them, were produced to the east of the Selkirks.

Subsequent erosion of the Selkirks has left the evidence upon which this conjecture is based. Ice, wind and water have done the final sculpturing. The product that we experience is the result of fluctuations of ice-ages, constant down-wasting, and the transportation of material by water to western margins of the North American continent.

That is the basic history of Nelson's Mountains, though over-simplified. The true magnitude of the occurrences and time concepts involved are hardly imaginable to the mind of man.

The region's ancient river valleys were first determined by the structural deformities, the great faults or breaks in the earth's crust, as mountain building proceeded over the eons. In patient trial and error, water has searched out the easiest possible down-grade courses through fault-formed valleys within the mountain ranges, and poured forth into the ocean at the edge of the continent. Though many characteristics of the Columbia River system were determined by the ice-ages, its course was basically established by the northwest-southeast trending structure of longitudinal fault valleys such as the Rocky Mountain Trench. The great lateral faults allowed an east-west passage through the ranges. These fault-formed valleys have further been modified by vast glaciers which filled and scoured the valleys, melted and deposited enormous amounts of material, creating varied landforms and distinctive features.

It is obvious a great combination of factors caused the gradual formation of the mountainous world of the Selkirks. Those factors relate back to the beginning of earth, to basic physical laws by which our globe was originally formed and continues to change. To understand why these mountains exist is to understand nature and its unending cycle of construction and destruction, life and death.

Just as all living things begin aging and face death from the moment of birth, so too do mountains face certain destruction from the moment they begin to rise from the ocean basins. If the forces that cause the upheaval continue at a rate exceeding that of erosion and eventual destruction, then a range of mountains begins to take shape over millions of years. As land mass rises, erosional processes form valleys and peaks. Rivers begin contouring the land, climatic conditions are altered inducing drastic changes such as ice-ages or droughts.

In the waxing and waning of ice-ages, glaciers leave behind lakes, outwash plains, massive boulders, soil deposits and other features. Rivers are often diverted, forced into new valleys or dammed up, apparently in total chaos. What we see is nature's final solution to creating order, the landscape carved and altered by the elements.

Mountain building is an ongoing and continuous battle between forces of creation and destruction. And if in our mind's eye we can see this awesome cycle of crustal rejuvenation then we surely must wonder about the powers of nature and comparable insignificance of man. In a world which has become contiuously more dominated and deformed by man, it is of no surprise that the human intellect becomes increasingly more fascinated by the forces which have created such grand monuments as the Selkirks - Nelson's Mountains.

Nelson's Mountains   *J. F. Garden*

19

THE
PURCELL
MOUNTAINS

THE PURCELL MOUNTAINS

Geologically similar to the Northern Selkirks, the Purcells are now recognized as a separate chain of mountains from the Selkirks. The range is defined on the east by the Columbia-Kootenay Valley better known as the Rocky Mountain Trench, and in the west by the Beaver-Duncan Valley and Kootenay Lake.

Today the Purcells are touted as having some of the world's best helicopter skiing, primarily in the Bugaboo region. The Conrad Icefield is the largest glacial area in these mountains, though not the only one. The Lake of the Hanging Glaciers, a remnant of past ice-ages, exists as a result of the scouring of great masses of ice which carved the basin, provided melt-water, and coloured the lake in hues of emerald.

These are only a few of the wild and spectacular areas in the Purcell range, much of which see very little human activity because of the remote nature. No major highways, railways or other means of communication traverse the Purcells, access being limited to logging roads, foot trails or helicopter. As a result, one is sure to discover a pristine wilderness area.

page 20
Dark-eyed Junco (Junco hyemalis)
M. Pirnke

Mule Deer (Odocoileus hemionus)
U. Veideman

CONRAD ICEFIELD

Flying south from Golden, British Columbia, a vast panorama of ridges and valleys unfolds below. Peaks of such romantic names as "Moonraker" and "Tetragon" rise above our moderate flying altitude. Below, are the Spillimacheen River and Bobby Burns Creek. Paralleling our course is Vowell Creek. To the southwest, a massive area enshrouded in perpetual snow and ice begins to overwhelm all else. This is the Conrad Icefield.

Central in the icefield is Mt. Conrad named in honour of Canada's most famous mountaineer and guide, Conrad Kain (1883-1934). On the northwest of this expanse of ice is Mt. Thorington which takes its title from the well-known author and mountaineer J. Monroe Thorington, a close friend and client of Conrad Kain.

To the south, we can see the Vowell Group and the vertical spires of the Bugaboos. All are incarcerated in the tight grip of a continuous sea of ice extending from Mt. Thorington to the Bugaboos. Descending from the icefield into the valley floors are the spectacular ice falls of the Conrad, Vowell and Bugaboo Glaciers.

facing page
Mt. Conrad and the Vowell Glacier
Flowing from the Conrad Icefield, the Vowell Glacier descends beneath the mountain named in honour of Canada's greatest and most respected guide, Conrad Kain. Mt. Conrad (10670 feet) was first climbed by Dr. and Mrs. Richards with Kain as guide in September 1933, it was Conrad's last climb!
R. W. Laurilla

From these glacial tongues are emitted the various tributary creeks which eventually find their way eastward to the Columbia River. The Conrad Icefield area remains tightly enclosed in the fist of winter for as much as 10 months of the year, receiving tremendous snowfalls as are necessary to cause the build-up of this vast icefield. It also brings delight to many skiers who forfeit fortunes to visit this snowbound part of the world.

As the snow storms come and go depositing layers of exquisitely shaped snowflakes year after year and century after century, the flakes settle and change from their crystalline shape to a more granular compact form known as firn, or névé. As compaction by weight increases, air is squeezed out of the firn or névé and ice is formed. The ice accumulates in thickness and lower layers reach a final plastic stage as a result of great weight and pressure. These layers tend to move or be squeezed outward from below the icefield, flowing easily along any downward course. As these moving masses of ice, or glaciers, begin to course downhill the resulting scouring of material along their route contours glacial valleys and basins, and ridges which gradually erode until only island-like peaks remain in a sea of ice.

In the Conrad Icefield, all these ice-age phenomena can be seen at work. The glacial tongues flow down-valley to the point where melting of ice exceeds continuous motion. When it is said a glacier is receding, motion has not stopped or reversed, but rather there is a more excessive ice melt at the glacial snout than there is movement. This is the case with the glaciers in the Selkirks and Purcell Mountains, illustrated by comparing photographs from the late 1800's.

The formation of ice and glaciers is another of

nature's unique processes, a vital part of the water supply and an erosional agent which alters the shape of the land. The icefields contain enormous quantities of water in their frozen reservoirs and emit a continuous supply. Their erosional strength reduces mountains to rocks, to gravel, to sand and finally silt. The silt is carried by the glacial streams and deposited afar, forming fertile bottomlands useful for agriculture. The icefields have also become recreational areas where man can enjoy nature and experience the all-encompassing beauty of the mountains, glaciers and silt coloured lakes.

We leave the Conrad Icefield and as we pass southward over the fantastic granite spires of the Bugaboos, along Howser Creek and Kootenay Lake toward the town of Nelson, BC, nothing seems as impressive as was the vast white expanse of ice broken intermittently by vertical rock and set off by a background of deep blue sky. All else appears inconsequential, though the colours of the silt-laden lakes reflect the influence of the great icefields, far beyond the reaches of civilization.

Piper Super-Cub C-FHCJ
April, 1980

facing page
Tetragon Peak   *J. F. Garden*

below
Conrad Icefield   *J. F. Garden*

26

THE BUGABOOS

In what to geologists is recent time, perhaps 100 million years ago, (300 million years after the initial warping of the earth's crust which initiated creation of the Purcells and Selkirks) violent breaks and internal swelling recurred along the Selkirk Ranges causing tremendous earthquakes, landslips and faults.

This action was conjunctive with the origins of the Rocky Mountains to the east. Within the Selkirks, an upwelling of molten plastic-like rock forced its way into weaknesses within the fractured earth's crust and the roots of the existing mountain ranges.

After a long period of violence and destruction, the plastic rock gradually cooled and crystallized, forming hard and uniform masses of granite. After an additional 70 million years, as the erosional processes removed the sedimentary rocks covering the granitic intrusions, these crystalline rocks became exposed resulting in the spires which we know as the Bugaboos.

Then man appeared, at first deep within the valley of Bugaboo Creek, then later on the spires themselves.

The first documented visit to the Bugaboos took place in September of 1910, by the Longstaff-Wheeler expedition. Dominion surveyor Arthur O. Wheeler, his guide Conrad Kain, photographer Byron Harmon, adventurer and climber Thomas G. Longstaff and outfitters Charlie Lawrence and Bert Barrow travelled by pack-train up a trail along Bugaboo Creek from the Columbia River. That trail was well known and had been used by miners for many years. The name Bugaboo Creek had long been used but the origin of that name is a mystery indeed.

Undoubtedly, trappers and prospectors had visited this area long before the Longstaff-Wheeler expedition, probably exploring for minerals and furs as early as the middle of the 1800's. In 1898, Wilmer C. Wells, a man of local renown was said to have traversed the Purcells in winter, travelling via Bugaboo Creek. However, there is some suspicion as to his route because the pass that was subsequently named Wells' Pass, later renamed Earl Grey Pass, is far to the south at the headwaters of Toby Creek.

In 1906 there occurred a small mining rush in the area. Prospectors had been exploring the valley for years and near the Bugaboo Falls a brown staining of sulphides indicated a presence of copper or galena. Then, at the headwaters of Bugaboo Creek, on top of the range's watershed a strongly mineralized area was discovered and staked. Many references to the Bugaboo Mine have been made, and likely, the naming of that mine resulted in the origin of the Bugaboo name.

Oxford Dictionary refers to bugaboo or bugbear, as "an object of baseless fear" or a "false belief used to intimidate or dissuade." Among miners a bugaboo is generally a blind or deadend mineral

facing page
Fred on Bugaboo Spire   R. W. Laurilla

pages 30 and 31
Moon over Marmolata
A spectacle of beauty unfolds upon the Bugaboos as early morning winter light begins to steal over the landscape, a waning full moon hangs over Marmolata as the new day breaks.   R. W. Laurilla

29

lead. It is possible that the mine on the Purcell watershed was just such a bugaboo, as it never amounted to anything worthwhile.

The Longstaff-Wheeler expedition of 1910 followed a creek named Bugaboo. They searched for peaks known only as the Spillimacheen Spires and were not at all sure that they would find them on the Bugaboo Creek. As it was, they were lucky, discovering a huge glacier on the north branch of the creek which led upward to the sought-after spires. They named the glacier Harmon's Glacier after its discoverer.

The Spillimacheen Spires were labelled in accordance with geographical terminology as the Nunataks, peaks or mountains standing isolated, totally surrounded by ice as islands in the sea. The survey was conducted from what was named Sextet Ridge to the south of the glacier, the Nunataks being recorded as Number One, Number Two, and Number Three, later renamed Pigeon Spire, Snowpatch Spire, and Bugaboo Spire.

In all probability, common use of the name Bugaboo resulted during the 1916 adventures of Conrad Kain, Albert MacCarthy and their climbing party. Naturally, Conrad Kain had been anxious to return to the spires since the 1910 trip with Wheeler and Longstaff; his sights set on climbing some of the most spectacular peaks he had seen since his days in the Alps.

On August 29, Kain and MacCarthy, John Vincent and Mrs. MacCarthy, decided to attempt the south ridge of peak Number Three, which appeared to have a reasonable line for success. Up to the 10,000 foot level, the climbing was straight-forward and enjoyable. Kain and Vincent climbed quickly while Mr. and Mrs. MacCarthy proceeded at a more leisurely pace. When they caught up, they found Kain studying a formidable gendarme which blocked their continued progress up the south ridge. A gendarme is a term applied to a pinnacle or block of rock which obstructs a ridge or arête. MacCarthy referred to this unexpected obstacle as a "vertible bugaboo" which suggested "the appropriateness of the name 'Bugaboo' for this spire."[1]

The gendarme, which was the crux of the climb, appeared to be a problem and as defined by the term bugaboo, was an object of baseless fear.

However, it took Conrad Kain numerous attempts and an hour and a half to finally push the route up and over the gendarme. With climbing techniques as they were in that day, Kain had virtually no protection save a hemp rope which MacCarthy payed out as Conrad ascended.

A fall was out of the question and yet the move Conrad made across the face of the holdless gendarme would today be considered a moderately difficult effort even with the modern advantage of rubber soled shoes, pitons for protection and tested nylon ropes. Using friction and little else, Kain inched his way over the rough granite reaching a slanting crack which led to safety.

MacCarthy relates, "Just how he finally got into the crack is a mystery to us, but after a dozen reappearances, he smiled and said: 'I make it'. He soon began to call for rope, until about 60 feet had run out and he called from the top of the ridge above the gendarme."[2]

The bugaboo though an obstacle, failed to deter their success and the south summit was reached at 12:45. The party continued to the north summit, finding it the same altitude as the south 10,250 feet. Their descent past the gendarme was completed utilizing a rappel (a roped descent using a fixed rope as a brake) down the backside to where a ledge of considerable exposure lead back to the south ridge proper.

This classic ascent was the prelude to years of exploration among the Bugaboo Spires, climbing which led to the eventual ascent of all the peaks and more amazingly, all the vertical rock walls of the severest difficulty. Conrad Kain remains highly prominent in the exploits of the Bugaboos, as well as other great climbers such as Fritz Weissner, Raffi Bedayn, Fred Beckey, Ed Cooper, Brian Greenwood, and Yvon Chouinard.

facing page
Bugaboo Spire
   Suiting the term spire, Bugaboo Spire (10450 feet) towers over the Vowell Glacier, with Howser Spires (11150 feet) rising impressively in the background. Both were first climbed in August 1916 by parties consisting of the MacCarthys and their guide Conrad Kain.   *J. F. Garden*

In the 1960's helicopter skiing began in the region and entrepreneur Hans Gmoser turned a dream into a reality. The Bugaboos became synonymous with powder snow skiing and spectacular beauty. In 1969 the government of British Columbia set aside an expanse of terrain surrounding the Bugaboos and established the Bugaboo Recreation Area and the Bugaboo Glacier Provincial Park. A mysticism has prevailed in the Bugaboos based on a fascinating name and on the achievements, aspirations and dreams of people who have been drawn to the challenge of these ice bound spires of vertical granite.

Boulder Camp
August 31, 1978

facing page

Anniversary Peak
Old fire burns are natural places to find Fireweed (Epilobium augustifolium). Here the flowers provide a beautiful foreground to the view of Anniversary Peak (9650 feet) which is on the south edge of the Bugaboo Glacier. *R. W. Laurilla*

Howser Towers from Vowell Glacier
Seen through the mists of a dissipating winter storm the three distinct towers of Howser Spire are appearing. This is the highest peak of the Bugaboos, the right or north tower is the highest (11150 feet) while the central and south towers are of equal elevation (10850 feet). *R. W. Laurilla*

below
Howser Towers from the west
The west face of the Howser Towers (11150') presents an awesome view of vertical granite columns rising over three thousand feet from the surrounding landscape. *U. Veideman*

Pigeon Spire
 Though one of the many Bugaboo Spires, Pigeon Spire (10250 feet) is very spectacular and distinctive in its own right. The east face is composed of sloping granite slabs at the bottom of which is the relatively small pinnacle known invariably as the Pigeontoe.

F. Duchman

facing page

Snowpatch
    The last conquered and most impressive spire of the Bugaboos is Snowpatch Spire (10050 feet) a peak that Conrad Kain admitted was beyond his abilities!   R. W. Laurilla

Cobalt Lake
    Amidst towering cumulus, Bugaboo Spire is framed by Eastpost Spire (left) and Crescent Spire (right) above aptly named Cobalt Lake.
R. W. Laurilla

Vowell Group
    North of the Bugaboos and the Vowell Glacier is a group of granite peaks, not unlike the Bugaboos, known as the Vowell Group. Snafflehound Spire (9750 feet) rises above Mt. Kelvin (9550 feet) (left) and the massive wall of Wallace Peak (9650 feet).
R. W. Laurilla

LAKE OF THE HANGING GLACIERS

Deep within the Purcell Mountain Range, 30 miles west of the point from which David Thompson named Nelson's Mountains, there is a unique ice age feature - the Lake of the Hanging Glaciers.

Located above the falls of Horsethief Creek in the backbone of the Purcell Range, still under the seige of the glaciers, this lake is of almost pre-historic nature.

It exists as a result of the glacier which actually terminates in the south end of the lake. The basin was carved by glaciers. The lake water is comprised of meltwater and the opaque turquoise colouring is a result of fine glacial silt precipitated from melting ice and held in suspension in the water. The lake basin itself is dominated by a massive headwall to the south, a part of the Jumbo Massif with peaks towering over 11,000 feet. Surrounding the lake are many hanging glaciers which at one time, prior to Thomas Starbird's discovery of the area in the early 1900's, reached into the basin of the lake and combined with the Jumbo Glacier to completely fill the valley with ice.

The lake's beauty and distinctive glacialogical features make it a living museum of natural history, providing a classroom in action which demonstrates the processes of the ice-ages which dominated North America. Its shores are covered in the flora of post-glacial recovery, flowers and scrub trees battle to survive amid a mixture of rock debris and sandy sediments ground up by the ice. A primeval stillness seems to overwhelm the visitor, though every night the air reverberates with sound as ice thunders off the headwall onto the glacier below, or calves off the ice wall into the lake itself.

Morning dawns stealthily, silently, with only the sound of a grating ice floe. Commander Mountain, the Jumbo Glacier and the Lieutenants headwall reflect off the perfectly still surface of the lake. The senses are bombarded by the idyllic setting of the whole vista. Straggling clouds float across the blue dome of the sky, often snagging the high peaks of the Jumbo Massif and piling up on the faces in an abscuring softness.

A sharp whistle rings out and echoes off the walls of the valley. The marmots begin their charming behaviour of whistling at each other from moraines and rock piles. As the sun shines between the clouds and warms the morning, bees and other insects crawl out from under the petals of alpine flowers where they weathered out the previous day's cool storm.

Climbing through the larch trees to the alpine meadows below the ridge of Glacier Dome, you can't help but marvel at the unending colours which saturate the meadows. Alpine flowers such as the Mountain Daisy, Alpine Fireweed, Buttercup, Heather, Fringed Grass-of-Parnassus, Veronica, Indian Paintbrush and the oft present Western Anemone create a virtual blanket. Below, the opaque turquoise water of the lake is dotted with ice floes and abutted on the far end by the ice wall and shelf of the Jumbo Glacier. The colour doesn't end on the alpine meadows! Perched on the limestone

facing page
Horsethief Creek Falls   *J. F. Garden*

Broad Leaved Arnica (Arnica latifolia)
J. F. Garden

ridge leading to Glacier Dome, where the view is spectacular, a profusion of lichen inscribes the rocks in a multitude of colours: orange, red, yellow and green! It is all part of the reward for the physical exertion of gaining the heights - the view of the Lake of the Hanging Glaciers and Jumbo group; the Starbird Glacier and pass with the MacBeth Icefield area and the Purcell Wilderness Conservancy to the west; and 11,000 foot Eyebrow Peak to the north.

Relaxing on the sunny ledge surrounded by an unending vista one wonders about life, nature, and the problems of mankind. In this spot it is mystifying why we should have any problems at all! Only the wind can be heard playing among the rocks, and an intermittent humming sound carried by the fickle draughts. But wait! That sound is certainly not imagination, but something like a drill, a portable exploration diamond drill! Sure enough, there on the shoulder of Mt. Maye, high above the Lake of the Hanging Glacier is a mineral exploration camp. The rocks around the valley definitely have that rust coloured weathering common to sulfide minerals and much chalcopyrite which contains copper, is evident.

Surely though, this place of unique natural beauty could never be invaded by mining interests. Hopefully our government could not possibly allow such activities to occur when so much natural heritage is at stake! Does not the destruction of this beauty and serenity mean more to man than profits to be made?

Was this visit to the Lake of the Hanging Glaciers an experience never to be repeated again or can those responsible for the mining exploration be persuaded this is a place of utmost importance in nature, of irreplaceable beauty which must survive the encroachment of man forever?

Glacier Dome
September 3, 1981

The Icewall   *J. F. Garden*

Lake of the Hanging Glaciers   J. F. Garden

THE
SOUTHERN
SELKIRKS

THE SOUTHERN SELKIRKS

The Canadian Pacific Railway, completed in 1885, and the Trans-Canada Highway, completed in 1962, both traverse the Selkirk Mountains via the famous and historic Roger's Pass. This route cuts through the spine of the Selkirks between the Mt. Rogers Massif and the Sir Donald Range. A most impressive sight as one motors the highway, is the south face of Mt. Tupper[1] veering straight up 4,000 feet on the steep north slopes of the pass and Mt. MacDonald[2] rising 5,000 feet in a sheer wall on the south slopes. The Roger's Pass is a mere niche in the chain of the Selkirks and because of the adversity of nature, the C.P.R. found it necessary to tunnel under Mt. MacDonald in order to avoid the continuous winter barrage of avalanches cascading down the sheer walls.

This corridor of communication is the arbitrary dividing line between the Southern and Northern Selkirks. The Southern Selkirks stretch southward to the Kootenay River at Nelson, BC and are bounded on the east by the Beaver-Duncan Valley and on the west by the Columbia River. Here are found the great ranges of the classic climbing years when C.P.R. guides used to take their clients up the peaks of the Sir Donald, Dawson, Bishops and Purity Ranges and the Asulkan Valley. Further south and extremely remote is the notorious Battle Range and beyond that, the Duncan and Slocan Ranges, and the Valhallas.

page 44
Rogers Pass Mist   *J. F. Garden*

VALHALLA

Like ancient ruins of a great cathedral built to honour gods of a lost civilization, jagged pillars of granite rise on either side of the enclave in spectacular relief. The nave of the cathedral, is a grand snow-filled basin which for a few months of the year reveals multi-coloured carpets of alpine flowers and jade tinted lakes.

As though built for the gods the Mulvey Lake Basin in the Valhalla Range evokes a feeling of sacred beauty - a distinct feeling among the Selkirk Mountains. No where else in the Selkirks are such magnificent granite walls found in such regular profusion, enclosing an alpine cirque so completely. The only route of escape is down a foliage tangled 2,000 foot headwall into the Mulvey Creek Valley.

As we took in the cathedral-like view from the col between Midgard and Gimli peaks which as of this July day had not yet been released from winter's grip, we talked of our tramp through a most magnificent piece of British Columbia. From Hoder Creek to the col on which we stood, we had viewed the wild granite walls of the Valkyr and Devil's Ranges and now finally, the grand spires of the Mulvey Lake Basin.

Here are rock faces which must surely rival those of any place in North America. The South face of Asgard was on our left, the West Molar facing, Gladsheim and East Molar beyond. On the wall of West Molar, Fred Beckey placed a route he described as improbable.[3] On our right stood the south and west faces of Gimli, the serrations of the Wolf's Ears and finally Mount Dag with its infamous Sweet Judy Blue Eyes buttress which took days to conquer. All are amazingly vertical granite walls ranging from 1,000 to 3,000 feet and are geologically a part of the Nelson Batholith formed during Cretaceous time, 80 to 100 million years ago.[4]

Along with the scenery, spectacular weather seems to go hand in hand with the Valhallas, as they are the highest physical features in this southern part of British Columbia. Certainly July proved to be no exception. Every day dawned clear but changed quickly with the buildup of cumulo-nimbus clouds off the surrounding peaks. By mid-afternoon, thunderstorms prevailed causing hair-raising experiences as when we found ourselves caught on Mt. Asgard.

An itchy scalp signalled the presence of electrical charges, then a buzzing sound surrounded the summit. I expected ice-axes and other metal to begin ringing, but as it was no time to loiter we scrambled down. Certainly, the presence of an electrical storm is an eerie and alarming experience on a mountain. Separation of ourselves from electrically conducting gear and escape from a position of prominence proved to be the only remedy to the situation.

For days, we thoroughly enjoyed the pleasures of the Valhallas and the Mulvey Lake Basin, however a toll was exacted in the end. According to our guide books, a trail existed down Mulvey Creek back to civilization. We chose this route of departure and descended the headwall below Mulvey Lakes into what proved to be an unmarked, unrelinquishing jungle.

Whatever trail once existed as marked in the cursed guide book, was now actually wiped out by

facing page
Asgard Peak   *J. F. Garden*

49

the great profusion of lush undergrowth. For 12 relentless hours, we battled and swore and endured the elements, including repeated downpours of rain. Finally, a trail did appear and we managed to escape to the civilization of Slocan City and the local establishment for a cold beer and a tube steak. For four days of spectacular beauty, we paid with one day of sheer hell . . . a small price perhaps for the pleasures we enjoyed exploring a place which will always be held with reverence as being a true Valhalla.

Slocan City
July 22, 1981

Midgard Peak   *J. F. Garden*

facing page
Mt. Prestley   *J. F. Garden*

50

THE BATTLE RANGE

Between the Valhalla Range and southern boundaries of Glacier National Park are a series of ranges little known and seldom visited. Of these, the Battle Range has long remained the most isolated and little violated wilderness area of the Southern Selkirks.

From Glacier House and the Roger's Pass, exploration of the Selkirks remains within a days walk until one attempts to reach beyond the Dawson and Purity Ranges. Prior to the advent of aerial photography, government maps of the Selkirks remained perfectly blank at the southern end, except for the words Battle Range printed on the unsurveyed region.

The origin of the name comes from a vague and legendary story of a battle between a grizzly bear and a prospector. Further details of the outcome of the struggle are lost, along with the identity of the prospector.

Three distinct clusters or groups of peaks occur within the Battle Range and they were named the Melville, Westfall and Nemo groups, again by anonymous explorers. The Battle Range has remained a remote and little explored wilderness. Difficulty of access had preserved the area without necessity of restrictive park regulations or other bureaucratic jurisdiction.

The Battle Range remains as it was in 1909 when Howard Palmer and E.W.D. Holway made the first recorded visit to the "country beyond the Purity Range."[1]

Palmer and Holway with plenty of time on their hands were determined to explore the unknown, to discover what actually lay to the south of the Purity Range, on the blank portion of the government maps.

"By our successes in the Bishops and Purity ranges we had pushed back the ranks of unvisited peaks not a little, and now there remained open from our base no more fascinating undertaking than a visit to the primeval fastnesses of Battle Creek valley."[2]

Proceeding on foot over the intervening ranges, Palmer and Holway crossed Asulkan Pass, descended onto the Geikie Glacier, then upwards again over Donkin Pass and Purity Pass before reaching the dark and deep confines of the Battle Creek valley. Palmer's words best describe their adventures as he recorded them in his 1914 book "Mountaineering and Exploration in the Selkirks".

"Dusk was upon us as we approached the crest of the high terminal moraine which had hitherto conceded the depth of the valley. For the last four miles, our route had lain through a forlorn waste of ice, snow, and jagged rocks . . . Accordingly, it was not surprising that we hurried rather anxiously toward the top. The scene which greeted us was indeed a wild one. Several hundred feet below a raging torrent framed out from beneath the glacier, racing into a narrow gorge with a thunderous roar. Lower down it emerged, and we could follow its course for perhaps a mile farther, winding between banks densely overgrown with alders. There the valley widened out and its gradients became gentler, but of forest there was hardly a patch. Alders and steep rugged slopes were the rule. Nearer, on either hand, its sides slanted abruptly back in rough rock-piles, breaking into cliffs higher up where ice edged the skyline and a ragged succession of sharp summits stood silhouetted against the evening sky.

facing page
Moby Dick (10460')   *R. W. Laurilla*

Just then what was our surprise to see, not 200 feet away, a fine yearling grizzly bear. He had been travelling in our direction out of sight below the moraine, and his astonishment at suddenly finding himself face to face with three strange creatures was laughable to behold. He stopped short, looked us over for a full minute, then gave a deep "hoowuf" and, turning around, disappeared. Regretting that our cameras were tightly strapped up in our packs, we continued down the gorge. We had progressed but little, however, when above us on the mountainside not far off, lo another grizzly was sighted, this time a full grown female with a cub . . . The old bear climbed over a snow patch among the alders, apparently to better reach their tender tips but the edge was too high for the cub, who could only get his front paws on it, so he hung there kicking ludicrously with his hind feet. The snow caving away presently, he tumbled down and had to seek a lower place. With no arms but our ice axes, and no trees for miles, it did not seem wise to disturb the brute or to give her any reason for desiring to make our acquaintance, so we slid down the slippery forefoot of the glacier to the edge of the torrent and pushed on down the valley . . .

Next morning we were up early to view our surroundings. In the darkness of our arrival, the heights had shown merely as dim shadows against the sky. Sounds of rushing waters in varying keys had reached us occasionally as the wind blew gustily down the valley, so we expected to see waterfalls not far away. Nor were we disappointed. Directly behind the camp a beautiful cascade leaped out of a foaming thread. Farther to the right, another gushed out, draining a glacier which was partly hidden in a deep notch. Fifteen hundred feet almost straight above this, a single Matterhorn-like summit towered in lonely splendor, forming with its lower and more distant slopes the eastern wall of the valley. The corresponding wall at our backs rose even more steeply to a belt of cliffs that extended for two miles along that side (west) and supported hanging glaciers as far as we could see . . . All in all, the scene presented the sharpest contrast

Nemo Group
From camp at Gobi Pass, the Nemo Group can be seen with Thumb Spire (9620 feet) jutting skyward in the evening light.

R. W. Laurilla

between heights and depths which we had seen anywhere previously.

There is little doubt but that the Battle Range on this side is one of the most difficult in the Selkirks from the climber's point of view."

Of the many peaks within the Battle Range exceeding 10,000 feet, Mt. Sugarloaf was the first climbed in 1890 by Forster, Huber and Topham. E.W.D. Holway returned in the summer of 1913 after his exploits with Palmer on Mt. Sir Sanford in the Northern Selkirks, and climbed Mts. Duncan and Beaver with the guides Feuz and Hasler and in 1914, Mt. Butters with Butters and Gilmour.

Little exploration transpired until 1947 when Mt. Proteus succumbed to N. Brewster and the Kauffmans. Peaks such as Mt. Ahab, and Pequod were climbed in 1958, Moby Dick in 1959 and Benito Cereno as recently as 1970. Such limited exploration is attributed to the difficult nature of access ensuring the security of the Battle range as a total wilderness for some time to come.

Moss Campion and Granite   R. W. Laurilla

pages 56 and 57
Pequod Glacier   R. W. Laurilla

Moby Dick Massif   R. W. Laurilla

Mountain ski touring - Battle Range
R. W. Laurilla

facing page
Typee Glacier   *R. W. Laurilla*

below

Beaver and Duncan
 Part of the Melville Group of the Battle Range, Mt. Beaver (10654 feet) (left) and Mt. Duncan (10592 feet) rise above this mountain tarn along the valley of Butters Creek.

R. W. Laurilla

AN EXPEDITION

In his 1888 explorations of the Selkirks, the Rev. William Spotswood Green of the Alpine Club, named many peaks and geographic features in the vicinity of Roger's Pass. The largest mountain mass in the area, just south of the Asulkan Pass, he named after the then director of the Geologic Survey of Canada, George Mercer Dawson. The initial ascent of this massive bulk measured at 11,123 feet, took place in 1899 and was achieved by Professors Charles E. Fay and Herschel C. Parker of the Appalachian Mountain Club of Boston, accompanied by two Swiss guides, Christian Hasler and Eduord Feuz. Fay and Parker applied the names 'Hasler' and 'Feuz' to the two main east and west summit peaks, respectively. Their route followed the Asulkan Pass from Glacier House, across the Geikie Glacier, up the Dawson Glacier to the prominent ridge which leads from Mt. Fox to the higher ridge between Mt. Selwyn and Hasler Peak, and on to the summit.

Today, Mt. Dawson is normally climbed from the mountain cirque known as Glacier Circle, which can be reached by trekking over land and ice. The mounting of a leisurely expedition to the Dawson group is the most enjoyable way of attaining the summits and of allowing the weather to give the climber a chance to realize his goals. At Glacier Circle the world is seemingly left behind. Not even omniscient jet contrails are seen, or any of the noises of our civilized world, only the sudden cracking and thundering of avalanches and icefalls,

constant babbling of mountain streams, or the hum of mosquitoes.

The route of ascent for Mt. Dawson from Glacier Circle, is up the lower ridge of Mt. Fox until the snowfield of the Fox Glacier is gained, then up the bare shale ridge exposed between the Fox and Dawson Glaciers. This leads to the summit ridge between Mt. Selwyn and Hasler peak. Either peak may be chosen from this point, but the highest peak (Hasler) is gained by veering right along the snow ridge and over a berg-schrund, which may cause difficulties, to the rock ridge summit of Mt. Dawson.

Below, is an unending panorama from the summit of this, the second highest peak of the Selkirk Mountains. The view is magnificent in all directions, but more so to the south, especially if one leans out to inspect the abyss that falls off directly to the Bishop's Glacier 3,000 feet below. Indeed to look south, it is as if an ice-age exists. Peaks such as Purity, Sugarloaf, Kilpatrick, Wheeler, Cyprian and Augustine in the Purity Range; Duncan, Beaver, Proteus and assorted others of the Battle Range stretch out below enveloped by ice draped over summits and ridges and filling the valleys between. In this primordial beauty the climber captures a glimpse of the world before man.

Mt. Dawson (Hasler Peak)
July 29, 1979

facing page
Over the Schrund   *J. F. Garden*

61

Illecillewaet Glacier

Flowing from its large névé or icefield the Illecillewaet Glacier descends between Glacier Crest and Mount Sir Donald. Once known as the Great Glacier, it descended far into the valley less than one hundred years ago.   *J. F. Garden*

Crossing the Névé

En route to Glacier Circle, three mountaineers crossing the Illecillewaet Névé indicate the scale of magnitude involved in their travails.   *J. F. Garden*

facing page

Mt. Macoun

Named after Dominion Survey botanist Professor John Macoun, A. O. Wheeler's father-in-law, Mt. Macoun rises some four thousand feet above the tarns of Glacier Circle. The tarns, or glacial ponds, are coloured by glacial 'flour-like' sediment held in suspension within the water.   *J. F. Garden*

facing page

Avalanche on Selwyn

Throughout the day, continuous barrages of ice and snow thunder off the east face of Mt. Selwyn into the basin of the Deville Glacier. Mt. Selwyn (11023 feet) is named after Dr. Alfred Selwyn of the Geological Survey of Canada and is itself the eastern peak of the Dawson Massif.   *J. F. Garden*

On the Summit

A world of ice and rock stretches out below and beyond the summit of Mt. Dawson. Beyond the triumphant climbers on Hasler Peak is the Bishops Range draped in ice, Mt. Wheeler and the Purity Range, and in the distance the Battle Range.   *J. F. Garden*

facing page
Deville Icefall
    The icefall of the Deville Glacier drops over a steep cliff some 1500 feet in height into Glacier Circle. It flows through a gap in the mountains between Mt. Selwyn and Mt. Topham from the vast Deville Névé which is named in honour of A.O. Wheeler's immediate superior Edward Deville, Surveyor General of Dominion Lands in the early 1900's.   J. F. Garden

Spotted Saxifrage (Saxifraga bronchialis)
J. F. Garden

ASULKAN PASS

On August 4, 1888, two English gentlemen of the cloth, William Spotswood Green and Henry Swanzy trudged steadily upward through hazardous crevasses to a col high in the Selkirk Mountains. Beyond the col was a scene of tremendous interest to the two - the valley they had looked into from the great snowfield (Illecillewaet Névé) a few days earlier.

"Our view was now across it at right angles. Some snow slopes flanked our col to the southward. Down these we quickly ran, and gaining a projecting knob of rock improved our view considerably. The Geikie Glacier, with a most wonderfully fissured surface, lay far below in the valley's gloom. From the Dawson range right opposite to us a most typical glacier, with lateral and medial moraines descended and just stopped short of being a tributary."[1]

Above the Geikie Glacier, and on either side of the glacier which flowed from the amphitheatre below Mount Dawson, stood the peaks which Green and Swanzy named Mount Fox and Mount Donkin in memory of two members of the Alpine Club who, with their Swiss guides, perished in the Caucasus.

While enjoying the view from the projecting knob of rock Green describes a noteable experience.

"We saw two white specks moving on the grass slopes below, which as they approached, we soon made out to be wild goats. Six others joined the

facing page
Mountain Goat with Kid (Oreamnos americanus)   *M. Pirnke*

first two, and came up to have a look at us, and then grazed without showing the slightest alarm. The long white wool hanging thick above the knee gave them the appearance of wearing knickerbockers. As we had no rifle they were perfectly safe, and Jeff, who was death on all kinds of small game, sat on his tail and looked at them with much complacency. They had never seen man or dog before, and Jeff had never seen that kind of beast except in the midst of civilization, and being a civilized dog he felt that barking at, or hunting goats would be the lowest depth of depravity.

There was now no time to make further explorations, so taking a last look at the goats we called the pass by their Shushwap Indian name, Asulkan, and picking up our light swags ascended to the col, and then trudged down the gently sloping glacier for a couple of miles at a swinging pace."[2]

Green and Swanzy returned that day to Glacier House on the railway line, their base during their summer long exploration and survey of the surrounding Selkirk Mountains. Five days later, on August 9, they ascended the great elongated peak on the west side of Loop Creek which Green had named in honour of Professor Bonney of London University's department of geology.

Their endeavours in the Glacier House area can be attributed to encouragement from Major Deville and Professor Macoun of the Geological Survey of Canada and the Royal Geographical Society of England. Green and Swanzy explored the great Illecillewaet Névé, Abbot Ridge, the approaches to Mount Sir Donald and the ridge of Mount MacDonald (Carrol) overlooking the Beaver valley, as well as the Asulkan and Loop Creek valleys and the summit ridge of Mount Bonney. Green produced a map of the area and presented it

along with a report to the Royal Geographical Society in March, 1889. Interest was so great that in 1890 William Spotswood Green published his classic account of a rough survey in the Rocky Mountain regions of British Columbia, "Among the Selkirk Glaciers".[3]

In 1899 famous alpinist Charles E. Fay also explored the Asulkan Valley, though his quest was

facing page
Asulkan Glacier   *J. F. Garden*

Snowbridge
The only feasible route to Sapphire Col over the Asulkan Glacier lay across a snow bridge which crossed the gaping abyss of a deep crevasse, on this day, August 20, 1980.
J. F. Garden

Asulkan Crevasses
The problems of navigating the Asulkan Glacier in August are obvious from this view of the Glacier.   *J. Maitre*

to climb the untrodden summits which lay in a long ridge on the west side. Above and over the Asulkan glacier, often treacherously navigated by the fortunate discovery of snow bridges over gapping crevasses, lies a small pass or col in the long ridge of peaks. Enclosed by the surrounding heights is a depression at the top of the glacier which is often filled with blue-green water, appropriately named Sapphire col. The name was applied by Professor Fay as his party was engaged in climbing the peaks. To the south of Sapphire col are the triple summits of Mount Jove called Castor, Pollux and Leda. North of the col is the Dome then Mount Afton and Abbot ridge. None of these peaks are of any great difficulty and the col in their midst serves as a most beautiful and convenient bivouac spot.

History lives in the names of these alpine valleys and peaks which attract so many climbers. Men such as William Spotswood Green, Henry Swanzy and Charles E. Fay left their mark on these mountains by naming many of the outstanding geographical features. They have admirably shared their knowledge of the unknown with all who have had an interest in the Selkirks - Nelson's Mountains.

pages 72 and 73

Pollux from Castor
From Castor, Pollux Peak (9186 feet) is impressively highlighted by the giant snow peaks of Mt. Fox and Mt. Selwyn in the Dawson Massif.   J. Maitre

Castor Peak
Rising above Sapphire Col and the Asulkan Glacier is Castor Peak (9118 feet). It is one of the three peaks which constitute Mt. Jupiter; Castor, Pollux and Leda. Castor and Pollux were in ancient mythology, the twin sons of Jupiter (Jove) and Leda.   J. F. Garden

74

BIVOUAC!

On a warm, mellow August afternoon in 1980 Jim Maitre and I set off on a long-planned mountain climbing venture. We had enjoyed successful climbing that season in the Selkirks and when on surrounding peaks in the area, our eyes were always attracted by the beautiful pyramid known as Mt. Sir Donald which rises strikingly above the Illecillewaet River valley.

We had considered ourselves a good team, perhaps no Habeler and Messner, but competent enough to attempt any major summit in the Selkirks with reasonable success. We each complemented the other in various aspects of climbing. I the better route finder, Jim the better at executing technique. Caution and sureness of protection was our mutual desire and if criticism could be levelled it would surely be that our cautions tended to slow us down when speed was of the essence. Our ventures have generally been of a leisurely and enjoyable nature and certainly we expected no worse for our climb of Sir Donald.

Solid quartzite rock - 10,818 feet in elevation and 500 million years old stands in a great pyramid dominating the spine of the Selkirk Mountains, about 45 miles east of the alpine town of Revelstoke, British Columbia. Travellers of the famous Roger's Pass route of the Trans-Canada Highway have probably seen this spectacular peak unless poor weather has shrouded the mountain, a not uncommon occurrence. The Sir Donald Range appears to provide an unpenetrable wall blocking all passage through the mountains at Glacier, BC. On the south end of the range above the Illecillewaet Glacier, stands Mt. Sir Donald which has attracted mountaineers since the area was first opened by the construction of the Canadian Pacific Railway in 1885.

Surrounding Roger's Pass is a mountainous area providing unending possibilities for the avid alpinist. From hiking to artificial aid climbing, it is all there in spectacular grandeur and challenge. Certainly some of the more classic climbs of Canadian mountaineering were experienced in this relatively small area. The most famous spot of all is the northwest ridge of Mt. Sir Donald. Originally called Syndicate Peak by Major A.B. Rogers, it was renamed in honour of Sir Donald A. Smith, chief representative in Canada of the Bank of Montreal and Senior Director of the Canadian Pacific Railway, who drove the last spike at Craigellaichie on the 7th of November, 1885.

The original name of Syndicate Peak was changed to Mt. Sir Donald by the government of Canada.

The Mountain was first climbed in 1890 by Swiss alpinists, Carl Sulzer and Emil Huber and their porter, Harry Cooper, via the Vaux Glacier and the south arête. It was not climbed again till 1899. To this day some years do not in fact record a climb on Mt. Sir Donald as its weather is notorious.

The northwest ridge route which was not established until 1903 by Eduord Feuz, Christian Bohren and Edward Tewes has since become the classic route of ascent. It is rigorous and time consuming but a most enjoyable route and challenging alpine adventure.

During the summer, Jim and I had set our sights on climbing Sir Donald and prepared by achieving climbs on surrounding peaks such as Mt. Rogers and Mt. Tupper. When the weather finally broke in late August following a week of cool, wet weather which left some snow on the high ledges, we decided to go for it! As winter

conditions are not unusual in late summer we felt this our only chance for a climb that season.

We found ourselves placing one foot behind the other on the trail leading to the base of the Vaux Glacier and the west face of Mt. Sir Donald. As we sweated our way up, we could see the menacing face of the mountain, wisps of light cloud setting off the deep blue sky above it. The weather was indeed excellent but still, snow remained on the high ledges, an indication of cool air.

Despite such a beautiful afternoon, we often glanced westward for signs of inclement weather heading our way, because by the following day we would be fully engaged in overcoming the northwest ridge. Up the moraine along the side of the glacier, on to green slopes below the west face of the mountain, over rock ledges to the col between Mt. Sir Donald and Uto Peak, we scrambled. On the flat top of a ridge connecting the two peaks, between

Northwest Ridge and Northface of Mt. Sir Donald　　　　　　　　　*J. F. Garden*

Sunset over Hermit Range　　　*J. F. Garden*

a vertical thousand foot drop and a pretty mountain glacier, we established camp. Now we had time to admire the view and prepare for the pre-dawn start up the ridge.

As we marvelled at the vertical pile of rock which we had set our amibitions on, we sighted a lone climber in an orange anorak descending the ridge. It was going to be touch and go whether he would make it down to the col by dark. As we watched his progress, the sun set over Hermit Range. It was breathtakingly beautiful and left one with the feeling that all ties with the real world had been severed. While all else was plunged into darkness below, the alpen glow rendered the cold rock and snow a warm golden orange.

A clattering of stones on the ridge brought us back to reality and the presence of our late arriving visitor. He reached our camp shortly after dark and rested with us for a while. Snow on the upper part of the mountain he explained, had slowed his progress considerably and caused apprehensive moments. Otherwise the climb had been a good one. Rather than stay the night he wished to descend to the valley so we bid him adieu.

On settling into sleeping bags, we were surrounded by nocturnal visitors - pack rats! These are bushy-tailed wood rats that love to eat provisions, chew rope and leather, and exchange objects pleasing to their eye with their own offerings. Needless to say, their enthusiastic scurrying hither and thither disturbed our sleep. We made sure anything susceptible was cached in the glacier snow which they abhored.

As I lay there listening to their activity, a projectile whizzed overhead, crashing into the rocks near my feet. Sparks and splinters flew accompanied by a string of vindictive words. Jim's temper had overcome his efforts at co-existence with these rodents. Things seemed to calm down somewhat after that episode. Quiet prevailed. Sleep came under a canopy of stars, beautiful to behold above the dark mass of mountain that stood over us, waiting.

As morning light spread over the ice below, we awakened in the cold of the pre-dawn and set to cooking a hot breakfast and making final preparations for the assault. The sun rose in a great ball of orange over the Dogtooth Range in the east and spread warm fingers of light over the Uto Glacier. When we turned west we were further charmed as the sun began to expose the highest peaks in a golden glow of early morning light while the valleys, still invisible in the depths of night, continued their slumber. We knew we had to get a move on, but stood transfixed for some time by the splendor.

Upon recovering from our trance, we climbed into harness, roped up, and began our climb. The rock proved friendly with hand and footholds where needed. There seemed a solidarity and cohesiveness often found lacking when climbing in the nortoriously "rotten" Rockies. As we climbed, alternating leads between us, a weather eye remained cocked on the western skies. High clouds in long north-south grey bands had formed and were arching their way in from the Pacific.

Although we agreed the first indications of poor weather may be moving in, we decided there was no threat to our venture - yet. We estimated a full day of good conditions and continued up Mt. Sir Donald.

We gained altitude on the ridge and the exposure on both sides became more and more impressive. At first, it was unnerving but gradually we became comfortable and in fact, quite blasé about the drop. On our left, the mountain was almost sheer with some broken ledges and blocks, down to the Uto Glacier. The vertical south face of Uto itself stared at us. To our right, the clean slabs of Sir Donald's west face fell off at a high angle towards the scree and grass slopes at the base of the mountain. It was indeed an incredible sight, not unlike a view from an airplane. The feeling of rock beneath our feet was however, more reassuring. To view the earth vertically before you and horizontally 3,000 feet below sends a chill down the spine at first but the climber adapts to his environs. Pitch after pitch the climbing becomes routine and the mind free from troubled thoughts, filled only with the thrill and satisfaction of overcoming the difficulties of the mountain. The actual effort of the climb is a joy. The view, companionship of friend, and beauty of nature is beyond compare. Heaven must be close at hand!

Over the first section of the ridge and on to the big snow patch we continued. Staying close to the ridge, or on the west side, the going remained

Sunrise on the Uto Glacier   *J. F. Garden*

Morning light on Mt. Bonney   J. F. Garden

good though sometimes a little treacherous as a result of the remnants of snow. It was not going to melt obviously, as the weather continued to cool.

The sky to the west suggested a continued deterioration of the day, if anything. After we arrived at the base of the pitch above the snow patch, we proceeded out onto the west face and up a small chimney, then up a vertical slab which afforded only a few handholds of good quality. With some exertion we managed this, the most difficult section, and continued upwards along the ridge proper.

We knew we were gaining elevation as we could look down at all the peaks in the area. Uto, Eagle, Avalanche and MacDonald, all mountains of some stature, seemed inconsequential to us from this altitude. The massive bulk of Mt. Rogers seemed the only respectable sized peaks from our altitude. To the south was the Illecillewaet Névé which stretched for miles to the base of the Dawson Range, from which reared the main summit, Hasler Peak, still higher than our own elevation. To the west was Mt. Bonney and though rather unimpressive from our vantage point, it stole our total attention. Wisps of cloud were beginning to collect along its leeward face, the sky was taking on a dark and threatening character.

After mastering the easy ridge below what is the final vertical effort to the summit, Jim and I conferred. We knew the summit was within reach, but time was against us! It was now 2 pm and though we might be on the summit by three, we faced another five hours of descent. Combined with the rather ominous looking weather it caused us to reconsider our continuing. Having had nothing to eat since breakfast and not having stopped for any sort of rest during the long ascent, we both agreed on a break while considering the situation.

We wanted the climb very much, especially as we were so close to the long sought summit. We had at least one strenuous pitch left to go, and were certain of victory within the hour, but at what expense? Time and the elements were beginning to pressure us. We did not desire a bivouac on the ridge, especially with that weather moving in and darkness expected within six hours.

We even considered gaining the summit and then descending via Terminal Peak to the Ille-

cillewaet Glacier, but neither of us were familiar with the route or the difficulties that might be encountered. Our camp gear was also at the Uto-Sir Donald col. With regret, we made our decision. It would be wisest to forego the peak and begin an immediate descent, in fact a hasty retreat, before the elements and the mountain conspired to trap us. With increased respect for the mountain and assurance that Sir Donald would still be here next summer, we began the long down-climb.

Filled with disappointment, we discussed the descent and the feasibility of rappelling to offset our lack of time. We gathered our slings, dug out our clog descendeurs and made the necessary preparations for a most thrilling descent. We also found it necessary to wear warmer clothes, as a thunderstorm was now advancing up the Illecillewaet Valley below us, a cold cutting wind preceeding it.

Off the big buttress above the snowpatch, we descended in quick and exciting order. The view below extended some 4,000 to 5,000 feet below our boot soles to the Vaux Glacier and the trail which we had ascended yesterday. Down-climbing past the snowpatch, back onto the ridge proper; our vertical view was 3,000 feet down to the crevasses of the Uto Glacier below the northeast face of Mt. Sir Donald. The col between Uto and Sir Donald, our goal, was still hidden by the ridge we were descending and we were not to see it as quickly as was hoped as the cloud and mist filled the valley below and swarmed into the col.

The sight of the mists spreading upward was very disheartening indeed. Before long we found ourselves sporadically engulfed in the mists. We could hear the echoed booming of thunder as the storm approached. We were now ever alert for signs of electrical disturbance: the buzz of metal or tingling of hairs. The sky was pitch black and suddenly, through the mists was a flash, followed by a loud crack and roaring bang of thunder! We took refuge under an overhang and stared into the oblivion of the mists, watching as alternating sleet and hail descended from above. In our vigil, we noticed that daylight was really beginning to fail, a dire warning that we had to get moving or face the undesirable necessity of homesteading on this abominable pile of rock.

The thunderstorm passed eastward and occasionally the mists allowed us a quick look at the surrounding environs. Though we did not appreciate the fact at the time, the mists blowing through the col below and enveloping the valleys provided a beautifully soft aura of silence, a wispiness of unreality, a feeling of immortality. It seemed as though nature would never be so harsh as to possibly do us in, demand our lives, or deny us a return from her realm. It seemed so soft, so forgiving, so menacing, that one felt like relenting, giving up forever the unbelievable, nonsensical life we lived down in the dark valleys below. Here was heaven and we were trying our damndest to descend into hell!

We rappelled as fast as we were able, but were unsuccessful in detering darkness, brought on earlier than usual by the storm.

As Jim was going over the edge on a pitch of down-climbing, I suggested we stay the night on a sheltered ledge. At first, he argued we should continue the descent as the col must just be below us.

I agreed but expressed my disaffection at descending without any light. Besides, I had discovered a good bivouac spot: a flat ledge below an over-hanging ridge on the leeward side of the mountain, out of the wind.

We knew the night would be terribly cold but having space blankets in our pack, made good use of them. Jim commented, in the past he had always wondered why he carried such excess junk - but now he knew!

We settled into our new home, an exposed platform about a thousand feet or so above nothing, at least from our vantage point. The only amenities were protection from the wind beating against the west face of the mountain and protection from most of the sleet by the overhanging rocks. We tried to enjoy our cold salami, cheese, mountain mix, an orange, and the last drops of water. To save weight, we had left our stove and soup below, a move we kicked ourselves for now. Our sleeping bags were also neatly stowed on the snow at the col!

I was situated in a crack about the width of my body. Comfortably wedged in, I wrapped up in my space blanket, using my pack for a pillow. Jim placed himself further along the ledge propped up in a corner under the overhang, fastened as both of us were to the bosom of the mountain with rope, carabiners and chocks jammed in cracks. We began a long, cold night's wait, a situation neither of us had expected or desired. But through bad luck and the quirks of nature, here we were!

We had taken calculated risks in making this climb. We had both pushed too far and perhaps should have retreated long before we did, when the first signs of bad weather appeared. If, through the kindness of nature and our own stamina, we were to survive this ordeal, we felt we would have endured in the will to survive the elements and in the will to live.

Nature relented during the night as if giving up on us for the time being. An array of bright jewels in the sky emerged, shrouded sometimes by the mists which drifted about the mountain. Another pack-rat made the evening more interesting, as efforts to ward off the cold were enhanced by energetic efforts to thwart his frequent visits! Finally morning arrived, as snow began to drift down from clouds banked against the northwest ridge. The mountain was not about to let us go easily. Because of the treacherous footing, it became impossible for us to descend except by rappelling.

Determination and careful work carried the day as Jim and I incredulously grasped the gravity of our situation. Concentration was aimed at safely getting off the godforsaken mountain, as more snow began to pile up on the ledges. Certainly, another night on the ridge would be the end of a

Yellow Columbine (Aquilegia flauvenscens)
J. F. Gardens

Descending in the Storm　　　　　*J. Maitre*

facing page
Storm on Mt. Sir Donald　　　*J. F. Garden*

lot of hopes, dreams, and aspirations. Through the mists, the col appeared below and to our tremendous relief the pitches ended.

A blizzard was blowing above timberline in the Selkirk Mountains and though whipping along with tremendous fury, it was also a thing of beauty. Everything was plastered with snow and through breaks in the storm, snow feathered peaks could be seen. Lower down, green trees were frosted with white. Truly a dramatic scene!

Once the battle with the mountain and the weather was over, reflection brought a sense of accomplishment. That brush with nature's fury instilled in us a feeling of reverence for the elements never realized until we encountered such an overwhelming experience.

No one attempts or desires to find themselves in such a fool hardy circumstance. But, afterwards we felt a heightened awareness and deeper respect for the natural world.

Mt. Sir Donald
August 25-27, 1980

Western Tanager (Piranga ludoviciana)
M. Pirnke

Orbweaver Spider and Web   M. Pirnke

facing page

Mt. Smart
   A little known blade of a peak, Mt. Smart (9527 feet) was named after the Deputy Minister of the Interior, circa 1900. It is visible from the Trans-Canada highway only if one knows where to look as only a brief glimpse can he had.   *J. F. Garden*

Eagle Peak from Glacier Crest. (9363 feet) center, and Avalanche Peak (9397 feet)
J. F. Garden

pages 88 and 89

Ross Peak
   Ross Peak (7728 feet) and Mt. Green (8870 feet) rise above the early morning mists on a warm winter day. Mt. Green is named after the early explorer of the Selkirks William Spotswood Green who, in 1890, published his classic book, "Among the Selkirk Glaciers". He also named many of the geographical features in the area including Mt. Bonney in honour of Professor T.G. Bonney who was President of the English Alpine Club at that time.   *J. F. Garden*

THE
NORTHERN
SELKIRKS

THE NORTHERN
SELKIRKS

North of the route of the Canadian Pacific Railway and Trans-Canada Highway, lie some of the most rugged and remote mountains of Canada's western cordillera. Here is the last stronghold of the grizzly bear in southern B.C. and here too, are the last virgin peaks of a range that continues to resist the incursions of civilization. Extremely heavy snows in winter and dampness in summer cause the valleys to be choked with underbrush and devil's club and the alpine areas to be laced with glaciers.

Here are the famous Adamants and Sir Sandford Range. Here too, are the lesser known areas of the Windy, Trident, and Remillard groups and others so remote that many days of bushwacking are required to reach them. Near Revelstoke is the beautiful Clauchnacudainn Range with its jewellike lakes and bountiful meadows. Adjacent to the Roger's Pass is the majestic Hermit Range.

Both Revelstoke and Glacier National Parks are located within the Northern Selkirks, though Glacier carries on southward to the edge of the Battle Range in the Southern Selkirks. These parks maintain a living museum amid the Selkirks, along Canada's busy communication corridor. Hopefully, the Selkirks will continue to prove to be bastions of wilderness and such potentially destructive industries as mining and logging will remain thwarted by the difficulties of access that these mountains maintain as their only defense.

page 90
Indian Paintbrush (Castilleja miniata)
M. Pirnke

facing page
Fang Rock
　　A spectacular peak on the west side of the Tangier River, Fang Rock (9302 feet) remained a virgin peak until 1956 when it was climbed by J. Burroughs and D. Isles in company with a man who has himself been instrumental in exploring and documenting the Selkirks, William L. Putnam.　　　*J. F. Garden*

Downie Peak (9891 feet)
　　A remote peak of the Northern Selkirks, difficult to climb because of its inaccessibility, Downie Peak fell to climbers only in 1959. The climbers were W.V.G. Matthews, D. Michael and no other than William L. Putnam. J. F. Garden

CLACHNACUDAINN

In the angle between the Columbia and Illecillewaet Rivers to the northeast or Revelstoke, British Columbia is a moderate range of peaks known as the Clachnacudainn Range. The height of the range is covered by the Clachnacudainn Snowfield, bounded by numerous peaks over 8,000 feet in elevation.

Unlike the native Indian names in the Selkirks, such as Illecillewaet (a very rapid stream), Clachnacudainn apparently refers to a great stone which served as the gathering and bartering place in the centre of Inverness, Scotland. The name was applied by Scottish stonemasons employed in the construction of the C.P.R., circa 1885. They also named other features such as the Inverness Peaks and the Gordon Glacier at the head of Clachnacudainn Creek. When Arthur Wheeler arrived on the scene in the early 1900's, these names were already established. In his book "The Selkirk Range", Wheeler refers to this group of mountains as 'Clach-na-coodin'.[1]

Though not as spectacular as the main ranges of the Rockies or Selkirks, this areas has been set aside as a national preserve by the creation of Mount Revelstoke National Park. Established in 1914, largely through the efforts of the people of the city of Revelstoke, this unique park is a beautiful preserve of alpine lakes and meadows, glaciers and peaks. It is abundant in the flora and fauna typical of the Selkirk Mountains and its gem-like lakes and multihued alpine meadows are among the beautiful vistas.

Hiking the trails in the Heather Lake area on a summer day, the flood of colours pervading the alpine meadows is astonishing. Indian Paintbrush, Western Anenome, Harebell, Shooting Star, Glacier Lily, Alpine Forget-me-not, and Mountain Fireweed provide a flowerbed of beautiful richness and colour. The sight of a Blue Grouse inflating his red necksacks and drumming away in his mating sounds amid the profusion of flowers and scrub evergreens, is common. A Whiskey Jack raucously calls out searching for handouts. The bird is often seen perched on the limb of a tree overhanging the rushing and splashing of Millar Brook. Suddenly, among the jumble of rubble from an old rock slide, comes a noise not unlike a bird call - "eeeeep" - the sound of a Pika, or Rock Rabbit. To spot this short-eared miniature alpine version of a hare or rabbit is very difficult as he is an expert at ventriloquism. His voice seems to come from one spot in the rocks, then another!

As the day closes one should remain for the sunset which occurs in a splendor of colour as the sun descends over the Monashee Mountains to the west of the Columbia River. Alpenglow bathes the Albert Peaks to the east as the shadows fill the Illecillewaet Valley bringing an end to another day in the Selkirk Mountains.

facing page
Millar Brook   *J. F. Garden*

Pika (Ochontona princeps)   *M. Pirnke*

Whiskey Jack (Perisoreus canadensis)
M. Pirnke

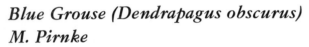

Blue Grouse (Dendrapagus obscurus)
M. Pirnke

facing page
Heather Lake Sunset   *U. Veideman*

FOUNDING OF
THE "CLUB"

In the valley which divides the Bear Creek watershed from that of the Illecillewaet's, where Major A.B. Rogers located the famous pass, there is a meadow of quaint beauty hemmed in by the surrounding vertical scenery. It trembles under the snows of massive avalanches in winter and shimmers in the multi-coloured splendor of alpine flowers during the summer. In this meadow, in the summer of 1883, the Alpine Club of Canada was organized. A.O. Wheeler, who did much to encourage its formation, wrote about the initial meeting.

"Here, seated upon a grassy knoll, amidst the very climax of Selkirk scenery, the meeting was held. What more appropriate! Around, in full view, are all the adjuncts that go to make alpine climbing of interest. The ragged black precipices of MacDonald and Tupper stand grim sentries over an apparently closed gateway. To the north and west, the primeval forest rises to grassy alpine slopes decked with brilliant flowers: beyond are icy glaciers and fields of pure white, sloping gently to the curving ridges that lead upwards to rocky peaks capped with snow.

The sharp-cut pyramid of 'Cheops' is silhouetted in space; below, the 'Little Corporal' stands at attention, on guard over the hazy blue vistas reaching into the southwest. Around, are gently swaying spruce and not far distant, a murmuring brook. Aloft, wrapt in silent meditation, the Hermit stands upon his ledge of rock, and gazes for all time upon the marvels of creations that surround him."

The club's executive was elected with Sir Sandford Fleming, president; secretary, Rev. Pincipal Grant; S. Hall Fleming (Sir Sandford's son), treasurer. A.O. Wheeler was appointed interim president.

In a dramatic gesture, the distinguished group of mountain pioneers turned to a nearby stream, rippling down to the Illecillewaet, and toasted to the success of their organization.

So was formed the initial organization for the promotion and instruction of alpinism in Canada. The Selkirks were the birthplace of the Alpine Club of Canada and fittingly, the man who surveyed and promoted the beauty of the Selkirks also became the guiding hand of the world respected association. It is also appropriate that a mountain of over 11,000 feet located deep in the solitudes of the Purity Range of the Selkirk Mountains, is named after A.O. Wheeler. He left behind the results of his survey and a remarkable history of the mountains he so loved, in his book entitled The Selkirk Range.

facing page
Alpine flowers   *R. W. Laurilla*

Monkey Flowers (Mimulus lewisii)
J. F. Garden

facing page
Mt. Tupper - Alpenglow   *U. Veideman*

Mt. Tupper - Fall
   Mt. Tupper (9239 feet) originally named "Hermit" after the figure that stands on its left hand ridge, was renamed after Sir Charles Tupper of confederation fame. Mt. Tupper stands opposite Mt. MacDonald and is the northern rampart of Rogers Pass.   J. Maitre

104

BALU PASS

A loud 'woof', sudden crashing and snapping of underbrush and a slight musty scent was evidence of the presence of a grizzly bear. And that was enough! That noise had sent our heart rate soaring and adrenaline flowing and it was some time before our bodies and mind settled down.

We had been strenuously labouring up the trail to Balu (pronounced 'Blu') or Bear Pass, when we disturbed a grizzly concealed in the brush off the trail. Unknowingly we had invaded his territory and were only thankful that he too was terrified by our presence. Had he wished to press the matter, the day would have ended at an early hour for us and likely on a tragic note!

One of the most infamous and highly feared residents of the mountains, Ursus Horribilus, better known as the grizzly bear, has been largely decimated by man and forced to retreat from far ranging habitats to high mountain valleys and inaccessible areas. The grizzly is still the monarch of the mountains, feared by all and void of enemies with the exception of man. It is said only the wolverine will stand his ground against the grizzly. But the grizzly is not a ferocious meat-eating

animal. He is more the self-indulgent brouser and scrounger, his curiosity often getting the better of him. Though they are territorially conscious and sensitive to invasion of their near-space, they possess interesting life-loving personalities, and have been observed indulging in child-like play.

I once watched one fellow sliding down the lower part of an avanlanche slope on his forepaws and rump, obviously enjoying himself. I have seen them drunk after wallowing and eating rotten grain from an old train wreck along the main line of the Canadian Pacific Railway. Unfortunately, such recreation is liable to get them into a mess of trouble as trains cannot stop to avoid drunken bears!

The grizzly is truly the most spectacular animal inhabiting the Selkirks. Their beauty in the wilds is fascinating. They are not however, an animal that can be easily observed as they are very shy and in fact, revolted by the scent of man. Chance encounters with these unpredictable, freedom-loving mammals are experiences to be remembered. With much caution and respect for their priorities, we can view them undisturbed in their natural environment.

We continued up the Balu Pass trail below the spectacular slabs of Mt. Cheops, and eventually arrived in alp-lands and flowered meadows. At the pass itself, we found a quiet lunch spot overlooking the Illecillewaet Valley with a view of the Lily and Bonney Glaciers, and Mt. Bonney which was shrouded in clouds.

While sitting in the lee of a lichen clad boulder, I heard a shrill whistle echo about the place. I whistled back as sharply as I could and another whistle answered. This continued, then other denizens of the meadow joined in the chorus and for

facing page
Mountain Daisies (Erigeron peregrinus)
  Mountain Daisies litter the slopes of Balu Pass beyond which rises the slopes of Mt. Cheops (8516 feet).   *J. F. Garden*

Brown Black Bear (Ursus americanus)
R. W. Laurilla

some time a whistling contest prevailed which must have left nearby residents of the hills totally mystified.

Such is the marmot or siffleur, who often basks on the rocks over his lair and emits such high-pitched whistles as warnings of possible danger. Hours can be spent watching and trying to befriend them, attempting to convince the varmints that you are not a grizzly who considers the marmots a great delicacy. Care must be exercised as marmots are quite deft at sneaking up behind an intrepid photographer and attempting to make off with an appealing rucksack of food. Marmots are another of the interesting fauna that are found in the alp-lands of the Selkirks and their presence is a special pleasure if they are willing to respond to your imitations of their kin.

After our noisy session, we shouldered our packs and began the strenuous plod toward the summit of Mt. Cheops. Struggling up slabs of scree and rubble, we finally reached the top of the long summit ridge only to be confronted by a pair of shaggy white creatures with startled eyes. Regaining composure, we watched in amazement as these two denizens of the heights - mountain goats -bounded down and out of sight in a flurry of tinkling scree. These extremely sure-footed mountain mammals, called Asulkan by the native Indians, are a very shy and fleeting animal. For the most part they do not take kindly to invasion of their domain. They generally spend their lives at or above the treeline descending to lower altitudes only during spring birthing and fall mating periods. Otherwise, little is seen of these hardy mountaineers, unless they are spotted on the high ledges and cliff faces where eagles frequent.

Banff naturalist Dan McCowan describes mountain goats.
". . . an exceedingly cautious creature, seldom taking a step until certain where the next hoofhold is to be had. A very short foreleg enables the climbing goat to hook his front hoof over the projecting rock and to pull himself up to safety. Further, the cleft of the hoof is unusual in form,

Marmot (Marmota caligata)   *M. Pirnke*

106

the open end of the 'V' being foreward. This is doubtless of great assistance to the creature when obliged to make a particularly hazardous descent over a smooth rock surface".[1]

The Asulkan Ridge, which we could now see from the summit ridge of Mt. Cheops, was aptly named for the presence of many goats in that area. Now however they are more often seen along the slopes of Mt. Tupper or on the shoulder of Mt. Cheops. Truly a spectacular and interesting inhabitant of the peaks, they are a challenge to photograph at close range because of their shyness and amazing mountaineering abilities.

On the summit of Mt. Cheops, a beautiful view of the Sir Donald Range awaited. On this particular day, the grand pyramid-like summit of Mt. Sir Donald was enshrouded in cloud. The peaks of the Asulkan Valley just touched the bottoms of the scudding clouds and Mt. Bonney to the south was completely blanketed with only the lower face visible. After a long sojourn on the summit, we made the regretful move to begin descent from our perch, toward the traumas of civilization. Rattling down the scree and broken blocks of

Nanny and Kid (Oreamnos americanus)
M. Pirnke

quartzite, we again reached the lower ridge called Balu Pass between Mt. Cheops and Ursus Major Mountain.

Descending the ridge to the pass, we were startled by a sudden movement coupled with a strange noise about three feet ahead on the trail. Almost invisible in the rocks and melting snow was a pair of Ptarmigan, one pure white, the other a mottled colour with brown feathers here and there indicating the change to summer plummage. They seemed very curious and were obliging when it came to being photographed. They are truly an alpine bird of the grouse family that rarely venture below the upper regions of the tree line. Though they seem very much the fool hen, they are always an interesting discovery in the upper alpine regions and remind us that life can be found in the most unexpected and seemingly barren places.

Boot-skiing down a snow slope from the top of Balu Pass to the meadow below, we continued on the path that led us back to civilization. Before us

Ptarmigan (Lagopus leucurus)   F. Duchman

facing page

Dipper (Cinclus mexicanus)   J. F. Garden

Asulkan Ridge
From the summit of Mt. Cheops, Asulkan Ridge appears momentarily through the clouds on a stormy day. The Asulkan Glacier can be seen with Mt. Jupiter rising above, the Dome on the right, then the Rampart, Afton and Mt. Abbott in the foreground, from right to left.   J. F. Garden

we could see the peaks of Mt. Tupper (originally named Hermit) on the left and Mt. MacDonald (originally named Carrol) on the right. The sun was declining and the late afternoon light bathed the peaks in a soft splendor of colours.

As we dropped further into the valley where the shadows were collecting, we crossed a creek below where avalanches had come roaring down off the east face of Mt. Cheops. We were delighted to see a very unorthodox and unassuming little member of the bird world which inhabits the shores and waters of the mountain slopes. Known as the water ousel or more commonly, the dipper, and hardly noticeable in summer, the bird can be easily seen standing on the white snowbanks in winter preparing for polar bear plunges.

Even in the dead of freezing winter, he splashes about open streams searching for particular delicacies at the bottom. The dipper is indeed fascinating and a very cheeful little bird emitting a pleasing note as he flies along the streams. He is proof again of the plain and simple joy of life.

Alas, we reached the end of our trail and of a very enjoyable day, one filled with the sights, sounds and activities of the alpine world. Life abounds all along the trail from the lush forests of the valley to the high barren summit ridges. The view from the summit was itself a most satisfying and worthwhile goal. It is no wonder then at the end of the day, tired and hungry, all that matters is what tomorrow's plans are for ascending the next peak!

Roger's Pass, BC
June, 1979

Western Anemone in seed (Anemone
occidentalis)   U. Veideman

The Major's Mountain   J. F. Garden

110

THE MAJOR'S MOUNTAIN

Mountain climbing is often considered a foolhardy risk of life and limb and always the question arises as to why anyone desires to partake in such endeavors. To each climber, different rationale, different feelings, and different reasons are entertained. However, it is not normal for anyone to engage in death defying feats of a daredevil nature. Certainly some risks are involved in climbing but with proper preparation, experience, and proficient companions, no more risk is taken and perhaps less, than riding in an automobile.

Undoubtedly, for avid climbers, part of the attraction of attaining summits is for nothing other than the splendid view and the different outlook one gets of the world. Some peaks, because of altitude or location, afford more spectacular views than do others and certainly, Mt. Rogers in the Hermit Range is one. It is a massive pile of quartzite rock which, along with its accompanying outliers stands totally isolated and higher than anything in the vicinity. It presents a view unparalleled by most mountains, with a 360 degree panorama for many, many miles.

The Columbia and Clemenceau Icefields are clearly visible 50 miles to the northeast. Mt. Sir Sandford and the Adamants stand to the north. Mt. Begbie and the Monashee Mountains to the west. The Bugaboos are visible beyond the monolith of Mt. Sir Donald and to the east stand the Goodsirs and Mt. Assiniboine.

The mountain is not a difficult one to climb and may be approached from a number of ways, one of which is the south facing ice slope between the peak of Mt. Rogers and the Swiss peaks. This is a spectacular, though easy and enjoyable route requiring only crampons and rope, strength and stamina. It starts with the ever necessary trek, then an enjoyable stroll over the Swiss glacier, up the steep south face, and along the final snow arête to the summit. At least an hour is required to fully appreciate the view and take enough photographs to satisfy esthetics, all providing the weather cooperates. The descent is as enjoyable as the ascent, what with spectacular views of the Sir Donald Range.

Mt. Rogers, named after Major A.B. Rogers, surveyor for the Canadian Pacific Railway, is a fitting memorial to a determined, tough and courageous man who thrived in the mountain wilderness. He is credited with the discovery of the famous pass which also bears his name. It is the only viable route through the Selkirk Mountains from the Columbia River in the east to the Columbia River in the west.

The major's peak was first climbed on July 30, 1896 by Philip S. Abbot, Chas. S. Thompson, and George T. Little of the Appalachian Mountain Club of Boston. The route they followed was up the prominent southwest ridge to the col between Rogers and Swiss peaks, then up the final snow arête to the summit. After arriving at the summit, Professor Little related,

"Mr. Abbot called me to its northern edge, saying, 'Look down and see what I have never seen before in Europe and America.' The sight was a wall of snow at least 1,500 feet in height that seemed perpendicular, as we cautiously peered over. From its base, a glacier swept away over an icefall, marked by huge irregular seracs, into the valley beyond. To us, toiling for hours over the blackened rocks, this sudden transformation of the peak into pure, untrodden snow, rising from a foundation of glis-

tening ice, was as startling as it was beautiful."[1]

On July 30, 1980, the view described by Professor Little was identical, and just as impressive! The Major, I am certain, would be humbled by the honour bestowed upon him by the marking of this particular peak with his name.

Mt. Rogers
July 30, 1980

facing page
Rogers Peak (10456 feet) J. F. Garden

Climbers on the Face ***Glen Boles***

Mr. Abbott's View
 This photograph of Mr. Abbott's singular view was taken eighty-four years to the day of the first ascent of Mt. Rogers. The weather from all accounts was similar, the mountain unchanged and the view as impressive!
J. F. Garden

CONQUERING
MERMAID

After studying guidebooks and maps and scheming with friends about undertaking a trek in the Selkirks, a decision was made to follow the watershed of the Northern Selkirks from the Adamant Range to the Big Bend of the Columbia River at Mica Creek, BC. Four of us set out on July 29, 1977 on an ambitious 18 day adventure into a mountain wilderness which soon proved to be beautiful and spectacular, but foreboding, isolated, and at times, treacherous.

facing page
Granite Glacier   *R. W. Laurilla*

The Adamants
In this morning view the main peaks of the Adamant Range stand spectacularly above the Granite Glacier. The Stickle (9950 feet) is on the left, then Adamant (10040 feet) and Austerity (10980 feet) on the right. The entire massif is composed of a dark granite providing for sheer faces and perfect rock for the climber.   *J. F. Garden*

pages 114 and 115

Rogers Massif
Viewed from the summit of Mt. Tupper are Rogers Peak (10456 feet) on the far left, the Swiss Peaks, Truda Peaks and right of the col, Hermit Mountain. The Swiss Peaks are individually named from left to right, Grant (10226 feet), Fleming (10381 feet) and Swiss Peak (10525 feet) after Dr. G.M. Grant, Sir Sandford Fleming, and the CPR's Swiss guides. Truda Peak (10226 feet) is named after Miss Gertrude Bentham, a well known lady climber of her time.   *J. F. Garden*

The holiday will always have a special meaning to our climbing party as we made, what we believe to be, the very first ascent of Mermaid Mountain.

Our first destination was the Fairy Meadows cabin located near the Granite Glacier in the awesome Adamant Range of the Northern Selkirks. On the morning of July 30, despite threatening weather, we made a start on our trek, over the Granite Glacier, then upward onto the Nobility Glacier to the col between Colossal and Enterprise peaks. From here, we perceived the sheer folly of our enterprise. We gazed over the landscape to the Remillard groups, and over what seemed a tremendous distance to the north, the Trident group. Certainly, we all had second thoughts concerning our venture, but no one wished to be a chicken-heart and suggest abandoning this project. As fog began to roll towards our vantage point we proceeded into the valley of Austerity Creek, crossed its waist-deep glacial chilled stream and thrashed our way up the other side of the valley to Austerity Pass. We descended into a mountain valley, this time the upper valley of Stitt Creek, where vast and comfortable alpine meadows afforded us a beautiful campsite for the night. The high cloud and mist above began to clear as dusk settled. We all craned in awe at the beautiful shapes which stood in vertical relief above us. These were the Waldorf Towers and the magnificent Whiteface Tower.

The next morning dawned clear, we packed our camp and climbed out of the meadows to a col on the ridge above called Craw Notch. We traversed the ridge to another pass called Nadir Notch overlooking the south fork of Windy Creek. After a brief repast we descended into the Windy Creek valley. Here, a small creek drained a glacial basin

to the west, which was the heart of the Remillard Group. We scrambled up from Windy Creek to a large boulder field above the glacial basin. To our amazement, a huge chunk of ice broke from the hanging glacier on the flanks of Remillard and plunged 600 feet to the small glacier below. A deafening roar followed echoing like thunder among the surrounding peaks.

After witnessing this awesome performance, we carried on through the morainal boulder field. As we skipped and scrambled our way through, tragedy was narrowly avoided. Stepping on an unbalanced rock, Roy Jones was subjected to a close call when the rock slid from beneath, pitching him into a hole and burying him with surrounding debris. We scrambled to his aid with dire thoughts of what condition we would find him in, after hearing his cries of pain.

Stitt Creek
Rising above camp amidst the mists are the Waldorf Towers on the left of the ridge and Whiteface Tower jutting into the clouds. No climbing record is available for those peaks of the Remillard Group, their inaccessibility and remoteness the reason.   R. W. Laurilla

facing page

Whiteface Towers
From the headwaters of Windy Creek, the Whiteface Towers present an imposing wall of spires and pinnacles resembling more a row of sharks teeth than mountains.
M. Pirnke

Remillard Peak
Part of the same granitic formation as the Adamants, Remillard Peak (9455 feet) presents an awesome north face towards, the valley of Windy Creek.   M. Pirnke

Remillard Glacier   *R. W. Laurilla*

facing page
Mermaid (9120 feet)   *R. W. Laurilla*

It took three of us considerable effort to lift the rock that pinned him down, allowing Roy to squirm out from underneath. Fortunately because of the size of the rock, it only pinned his legs rather than settling completely on our hapless companion. We felt relieved when bruises were all that resulted, but on the nearest meadow, we established camp and there remained for two days of rest and recuperation.

On August 3, well rested and non-the-worse-for-wear, we set off to the north of camp, up a ridge consisting of a series of peaks known as the Yardarm Ridge. We climbed to a high point of peak number one, and descending along the small north ridge, found we had to rappell off the west side of the col between peaks number one and number two, because of a difficult ribbon of rock on the latter's south ridge. We managed to traverse below peak number two and number three, and further on established a high camp 300 feet below the summit of peak number three. As it was close by, we scrambled to the summit sans packs and gear and enjoyed a beautifully clear sunset over Argonaut Mountain to the northwest.

The next morning, we continued along Yardarm Ridge to a col below Onderdonk Mountain. When we tried to ascend this pile of vertical scree,

we agreed it just wasn't worth the effort. Traversing again, we made our way along the east side of Onderdonk Mountain and arrived at a col between Onderdonk and the next northern-most peak known as the Mermaid, where we established another high camp. To date, we had left all civilization far behind us and solitude was all we knew outside of our own companionship. As we sat on the ledges of our camp enjoying the scenic grandeur, a helicopter came along, sighted our campsite and landed, believing us to be geologists the pilot was supposed to transport. After disappointing him and trying to explain our surprising existence there, he continued on his errands.

The next day the weather continued to co-operate and we made what we believe to be the very first ascent of the Mermaid. The climb consumed some four or five hours with some interesting roped pitches on good rock. The Mermaid rewarded us with a spectacular view of the Adamants and Sir Sandford, Mt. Columbia and the Twins along with the Columbia Icefields to the east.

In early morning, we broke camp and began an arduous climb to a small col on the west side of the Mermaid. After reaching it, we gaped down into huge holes and crevasses which we had to negotiate in order to descend into the valley of the north fork of Windy Creek. We had no choice but to descend. The only other alternative was to grapple with a horribly contorted and rotten peak to the west. However, we successfully negotiated the glacier with no problems and gained a large ridge system on the far side of the basin which led on to the Trident Group. En route, we met two geologists from Carlton University engaged in rock sampling and mapping. Not unexpectedly, they were considerably surprised at seeing other human beings in the area. We established camp near their site and spent an enjoyable evening recounting tales and experiences over an excellent, albeit basic dinner.

Continuing along the massive northerly trending ridge all the following day, we made a high camp below a small summit just south of Escarpment Peak. Here, we found we weren't alone as some curious resident goats clambered about the rocky ridges trying to get a better look at the unexpected intruders. It was with great interest that we watched them leap and run along the crags silhouetted by the evening light.

During the night, bad weather crept in and we awoke to a light drizzle - the first serious change in the weather since we had begun our trek. Our gear was stowed quickly to avoid a soaking and we began our day's efforts. The route we chose was rather difficult, but seemed our only clear choice. We had to surmount the small summit near which we had encamped, then make several rappells down to a small glacier on the northeast side of the ridge, cross the glacier and descend into the valley. There, it turned out, the bushwacking through alder was the most strenuous effort of all. Persevering, we gained sanctuary at the foot of the Trident Icefields where bare slabs and a large moraine finally allowed us to escape the soaking of the slide alder. Finding a small meadow alongside the moraine, we called a halt, established a camp, and escaped from wet clothes into dry, warm sleeping bags.

Dawn brought a clear beautiful day though we had slept in and were late to realize it. The sun soon warmed our tents and caused us to crawl out like groundhogs to bask in its warmth. Out came the foam pads, sleeping bags and wet clothes, then sunglasses and sun cream. We felt we deserved this luxury of relaxation and took advantage of the situation.

The following morning, however, four insignificant souls marched up the icefield, pouring out sweat in an effort to gain the col between Mt. Neptune and Mt. Dolphin. Here, at 9,300 feet, we could look west into a magnificent glacial valley which was the headwaters of Bigmouth Creek. We started down what was a very steep gully full of rubbly rock in the upper part and snow in the lower, our only route of descent on the west side of the ridge from the col. During the descent of the lower half of the gully, a sudden whir and sounds like whip cracks indicated a volley of rocks from the heights. We dived for what cover we could scrimp and huddled under our packs, waiting for the worst. It felt like being caught in enemy fire - not knowing where to go! We got away luckily again though, with only minor injuries, a little blood drawn.

Once onto the glacier, things went more quickly. We managed to reach the tongue of the ice in short order then crossed the small moraine to the

Mountain Bluebird (Siala currucoides)
M. Pirnke

facing page
South face of Mermaid (first ascent)
R. W. Laurilla

123

only meadow in the immediate vicinity. This was camp.

In the early morning light of August 12, we traversed westward along the flank of Trident Peak which towered above us and managed to gain a ridge system that came from the north in the direction of the Big Bend. Across the valley of Bigmouth Creek, was a remarkable and large glacier descending from the western side of the Trident Group northwest of Neptune Peak. It descended below the level of the usual glacial tongue, reaching right into the trees of the Bigmouth Valley to the 4,300 foot elevation. It was an amazing and beautiful sight indeed!

Summer home   *R. W. Laurilla*

facing page
Camp   *R. W. Laurilla*

On Neptune Glacier   *M. Pirnke*

Moving north along the ridge system through the remainder of the day, we came upon several small ponds which proved not unbearably cold. We camped next to one that was snow-bound and treated ourselves to a swim match and much needed bath, polluting the waters of a virgin mountain tarn.

The following day, we had to descend into the valley below us, foregoing the easy alpland hiking for the miserable bushwhacking which is unavoidable in the creek valleys. We crossed the valley and ascended to a ridge above the headwaters of the north branch of Bigmouth Creek in order to gain access to the northeast mountain area. Once on the ridges, we established a lovely high camp, overlooking all the surrounding country, making the day's efforts worthwhile.

Our route next day, was up and over the large glacier on the right flank of Northeast Mountain, over the ridge and down the other side over yet another large body of ice. We eventually reached the extent of the glacier and traversed sloping mountain meadows reaching the south entrance

Northeast Mountain (9909 feet)
R. W. Laurilla

facing page
Anemone Pass Camp   *M. Pirnke*

Tarn on Cornice Mountain   *R. W. Laurilla*

of the Anenome Pass basin. Here, we found an overwhelmingly beautiful and fragrant mountain alpland. Rolling meadows, small lakes, and countless alpine flowers flooded our field of vision. Here was utopia! We managed to advantageously locate our camp with a convenient lake in our front yard, and a view to the south of the 10,150 foot Mount Chapman!

Lazing in our surroundings, on the following day we felt motivated to do little more than relocate our camp to the west side of the Anenome Basin. We did nothing but stroll over the basin, admiring the continuously changing view of the

surrounding area. Just behind our new camp, was Cornice Mountain, our next objective and obstruction on our trek to Mica Creek.

Setting out on our final day, we reluctantly left the beauty of Anemone Pass Basin and climbed up and over Cornice Mountain where we had our first look down into the Mica Creek Valley to the Columbia River. From the top of Cornice Mountain, we traversed over to the top of Fred Laing Ridge in order to avoid bushwhacking down the south fork of Mica Creek. The ridge was a wonderland of its own, holding several small lakes where a herd of goats resided. After lunch on top of the ridge, we moved down along it where we discovered a profusion of Indian Paintbrush, the likes of which we had never seen before! Thirty-three distinct shades of colour were counted and the meadow was akin to a large bouquet fit only for presentation to royalty.

After departing from the fantastic colours, we began our descent from that unreal and ephemeral world of the alplands to the depths and dark-ness of a semi-tropical forest which included devil's club some eight feet tall! Navigation was difficult in the depths and we unwittingly erred by descending into the creek bottom instead of staying higher on the ridge. This caused great hardships in bushwhacking! Some five and a half hours of cursing, cloth-ripping agony later, we finally reached civilization and the townsite of Mica Creek, BC. It was 9:50 PM on August 16, 1977! We had made it!

Needless to say, we were glad to have arrived back in civilization, especially after the last agonizing hours of effort. It was into a shower, a quick cold beer at the local pub, then 11 hours at horizontal hold in the Mica Creek Motel.

That ended one great trip for the four of us, a remarkable trip in hindsight. We had only two and a half days of bad weather, the rest being sunny and clear, in some of the most remote country anywhere on earth. What more could we have asked for?

facing page
Fred Laing Ridge   *M. Pirnke*

Devils Club (Oplopanax horridum)
J. Maitre

Graham Matthews
Roy Jones
Mike Pirnke
Roger Laurilla
August, 1977

MT. SIR SANDFORD
and the ADAMANTS

Named for Sir Sandford Fleming, Chief Engineer and surveyor of the Canadian Pacific Railway from 1871 to 1881, Mt. Sir Sandford (11,580 feet) is the monarch of the Selkirks.

A huge and solitary mountain of terrific mass, it is located between Palmer Creek and the Gold River, south of the Adamant Range. It was first climbed in 1912 by the most noted Selkirk explorer, Howard Palmer. He was accompanied by E.W.D. Holway and guides Rudolf Aemmer and Eduord Feuz. Between 1908 and 1911, Howard Palmer had made five attempts at ascending this mountain, but only after an exceptionally mild, snowless winter and a warm, dry spring did Mt. Sir Sandford relent.

It must be appreciated that during Palmer's time no easy access to the mountains of the Selkirks was available. Five days of bushwhacking alone was necessary to approach this mountain, and then, as if Mt. Sir Sandford was not enough of an accomplishment, this intrepid party continued on to complete the first ascent of Mount Adamant (11,040 feet).

As Howard Palmer's own eloquent style reflects more clearly his climbs and experiences, the following account of his 1912 adventures on Mt. Sir Sandford and Mount Adamant was taken from his book "Mountaineering and Exploration in the Selkirks", published in 1914.

He wrote that June 24, 1912 dawned clear and warm though the valleys were hazy with the smoke of burning forest fires. Half-way up the flanks of the mountain on the northern exposure, Holway and Palmer with their Swiss guides Aemmer and Feuz had already ascended to a considerable altitude when the lanterns were doused and daylight illuminated their way.

"Continuing without any real delay, we retraversed our familiar route over the glacial plateau behind the Ravelin, up the slope leading to the snowy shelf, and then along the shelf itself. The passage of the interlocking bergschrunds was exciting work, for we found little snow to aid us and a zig-zag staircase had to be chopped out in the steep ice. The temperature had evidently not fallen below the freezing point since water was running everywhere. As a result, the snow on the shelf afforded heavy going until it got thick enough to support us well above its watery underlayers. Even then, one or another would occasionally plunge in above his knees, delaying the line while he extricated himself. In this fashion we plodded along until at 0505 AM we found a suitable halting place at the foot of the large buttress . . .

The barometer showed a rise of about 3,000 feet from camp, making the altitude approximately 8,700 feet . . . As we progressed, the traverse to the dome-topped rock, which had been hidden previously, came into view and looked perfectly practicable. Other conditions as well confirmed us in the opinion that this was the best route to adopt. Close inspection of the ice cliffs indicated that the glacier was not discharging avalanches with any frequency. The cleavage surfaces appeared to be rounding rather than freshly cut, and although here and there moderately large fragments almost ready to fall could be picked out, there was an entire abscence of the soft but incessant crackling sounds from beneath the glacier

facing page
The Hourglass   **Glen Boles**

pages 132 and 133
Mt. Sir Sandford (11580 feet)   **Glen Boles**

which had been so audible on our last visit and had then prompted us to discard the route.

. . . so without discussion we effected a passage over the crevasse and headed for the threatening cliffs. Aemmer kept up the slope to the right as long as possible in order to avoid the channel worn out by falling fragments, but at last there was nothing for it except to break cover and cross the line of fire to the farther rocks. Now the snow underfoot became hard and rough from the impact of tumbling masses and almost every step had to be cut. The only sound was the continuous pick, pick of the axe as Aemmer bent to his task. Mere scratches were all that could be afforded, but these Feuz enlarged whenever it seemed necessary.

'Keep one eye up there,' he exclaimed, turning to me for an instant and nodding toward the crystal wall. I needed no prompting, for my eyes had been glued to the cliffs for sometime. One piece in particular, about the size of a hogshead, claimed my attention since it projected somewhat and seemed on the verge of dropping off. If it had we could hardly have escaped the thousand pieces into which the rocks would have shattered it. Luckily the slant was gentle, somewhere about 30 or 35 degrees, so that there was little distraction on this account. Lower down, however, the declivity steepened into a giddy drop over the line of ice cliffs which edged the shelf. Incentive to maintain solid footing, therefore was not lacking . . .

Now we are at the rocks. They are round and smooth from the grinding of the ice but the foothold is sufficient. Aemmer loosens a few cakes of ice from the crevices and is up in a twinkling. The hard part is over. Not so the danger, for ice blocks are scattered all about on the ledges. We others swarm up as best we can, yet not without scratching of boot nails and whanging of ice-axes against the rocks as to call forth echoes from the grim, greenish cliffs. Next ensues a rough-and-tumble run along a rocky shelf to its outer extremity where safety awaits. As expected, it turned out to be the broad top of the domed buttress and by common consent a brief respite was decreed."

They were three-fifths of the way up Mt. Sir Sandford by 6:30 AM, with 2,000 feet left to conquer. A beautiful, hot day ideal for their venture was presenting itself and the party's spirits were high, though Palmer admits none of them took the climb's potential hazards for granted.

They decided to ascend a spur of ice to gain access to the icefield behind the dangerous cliffs.

"The ice, though broken, was not steep and only a little axe work was required to land us safely on the broad expance of undulating snow that covers the summit ice-field in a mantle of solid white. It seemed to stretch upwards and outwards interminably, for glittering battlements and leaning towers of ice on the sky-line cut off the view overhead and neither rock nor ridge suggested a boundary anywhere else. But the route, as we knew from previous inspection, led to the right in a long gently ascending traverse, so no time was lost in turning our steps in this direction.

For the most part, this portion of the way proved to be merely a straightforward, though fatiguing, walk through soft snow. At two points, however, we encountered rather large crevasses that held us up temporarily. The first ran directly down from the upper area of broken ice to the hanging glacier beneath us, being well opened and without a bridge. It was too wide to reach across with an axe, so Feuz, after selecting a soft-looking place on the farther side, executed a near flying leap and landed safely on all fours. The rest of us then followed his example, not without a secret misgiving, I fear, as to the procedure to be employed in getting back later, for the side we had just left was considerably higher. However, comforting ourselves with the thought that in mountaineering, 'sufficient unto the hour is the difficulty thereof,' we continued. The second crevasse, being higher up, was still fitted out with bridges so that no violent gymnastics were needed in this case. The motion was rather that of an Indian brave on the warpath shadowing an enemy, or of a cat walking through wet grass.

In this neighborhood, we began to open up views of various familiar features of the mountain. Just beneath us was the top of the small buttress that had so often been the goal of vain efforts past. Its steep ice-slopes was now practically bare of snow, and we could see to good advantage by what a narrow margin wind and cold had triumphed over us. Above and farther back, the frosty brow of Sir Sandford's ponderous southerly buttress peeped out, with the final arête, sharp-cut against the glowing sky, swinging ever upwards from the crest.

Altering our line of march thither, it was not until nine o'clock that we actually plowed over the edge onto the broad flat top of the buttress and came face to face with the immense panorama to the south. Naturally, our first concern was the nature of the remainder of the way to the summit, but one glance thither sufficed to dispel apprehension. True, the ridge was badly corniced in both directions, but it did not look at all difficult and not one of us had a suspicion of the actual obstacles in store."

A 30 minute rest followed before the climbers set out towards the south peak. However, an easy route was not guaranteed, as they soon discovered.

". . . We now perceived that the arête was like a long irregular wall, that it was piled up high on the top with snow which overhung for a great distance on the north and sloped down steeply to the edge on the south, and that our only possible route lay along this very slope. At first all went well, but as we progressed, the slope steepened and the condition of the snow grew worse. Soft and slushy from its full exposure to the glaring sunlight, it not only afforded the scantiest of holds, but at the same time exhibited a decided tendency to slip off the substratum of hard ice upon which it rested. Aemmer was constantly forced to dig away the snow and cut footholds directly in the ice itself. Not entirely pleasant was it to watch the fragments thus loosened start down the slope, disturbing more snow as they gained headway, until finally far below, a full-sized avalanche poured over the cliffs.

Under such impediments, a party's progress is like that of a garden snail, yet in time even this becomes surprisingly effective. The turns of the scalloped parapet kept falling behind us, but still the summit remained pertinaciously hidden. At length when nearing a rocky jutting promontory buttressed by high cliffs below, we felt certain that its disclosure could no longer be postponed. A moment more and Aemmer was on the knob, peering around the edge of slanting snow that formed our skyline. Not a word of encouragement did he vouch safe, however, but instead commenced a lively interchange of Swiss patois with Feuz who at once moved up and joined him in an intense study of what lay ahead. Standing room being limited, Aemmer presently cut himself a niche in the ice higher up which allowed me to advance. 'There is a nasty place here,' said Feuz, when I arrived, and nasty enough it looked . . .

Above this sheer face, an ugly-looking cornice depended. From the top a large mass of soggy, melting snow had just fallen, and water was dripping down like a shower bath. Clearly there was no way up there. On our own level, along the line of junction between snow and rock, the two came together so nearly flush that all chance of passage seemed utterly hopeless, while immediately beneath us a cautious look revealed smooth, ice-coated rocks ending in a tremendous snowy slopes which shot the eye directly into the valley, a mile below, but scarcely calculated to afford much assistance to the matter in hand."

While Palmer admitted discouragement during this portion of the climb, he writes; Aemmer as if energized by their previous lack of success, continued on.

"We held our breath as we watched him, for, to all intents and purposes, he was on the brink of

page 136
Mt. Adamant
   The route that Palmer's party embarked upon is the obvious snow couloir in the center of the mountain. Its objective dangers are obvious!   Glen Boles

Summit of Mt. Sir Sandford   *Glen Boles*

eternity. If another piece of that cornice should fall . . .

At length, nearly all of the one hundred foot rope was out and it was time for the next man to follow, so moving up to Feuz, I tied myself onto the end. Aemmer now had fairly good footing on the sloping rock but still lacked axe or hand-hold to serve as a quick grip in case of need. Nevertheless, the most hazardous part, the actual construction of the path was over. The evil spell of the place was broken to that extent. Surely, after such a gallant exhibition of pluck and skill in making of a way, it would be ungracious to balance the pros and cons of safety too nicely, so I started off, Aemmer cautiously taking in the rope as it slacked. Of the next few moments I have but a vague recollection. I know that the first steps were extremely difficult to negotiate owing to a soft, bulging boss of snow beneath which one had to duck sideways making at the same time a long stretch into a small ice step full of water beyond. After this, came a stride onto an outward-sloping bit of smooth rock for which the balance could only be maintained by thrusting one's hands straight into the snow. Then the wall eased off, allowing one to stand upright and to face forward once more. The ensuing steps were on the slushy outward-rounding rim of rock, a matter of careful balance merely, and not many minutes elapsed before I stood beside Aemmer on the rocks. While passing beneath the cornice, I heard a vicious swish just behind me which they said was due to about a bucketful of falling snow - a somewhat thrilling escape . . .

But the summit was not far away, because we could see a bit of its cornice above the arête ahead, so roping up at once, we started towards it. All of a sudden, we looked down upon the ridge that rises gently from the pointed easterly gable, and I knew that the culminztion of the four-year siege was at hand. Aemmer now redoubled his precautions, for evidently the actual top was on the cornice that jutted out a goodly distance into space on north and east and he desired to get as near as possible without leaving 'terra firma.' "

Finally he came to a halt and driving in his axe said: "Here is the top."

Two days later, on June 26, the party ascended Mount Adamant via a long and difficult couloir. Six hours were required to ascend the couloir which was severely clogged with snow and ice. Eventually, however, the party reached the granite of the final summit and were on top by five o'clock. They quickly began the descent.

"The hour was only nine, yet to all appearances it might have been midnight. Around about us great dim shapes loomed up through the rainfog, breathing forth cloud plumes from each turret and crag. Occasionally thunder muttered in the distance or rattled near at hand in short staccato crashes like musketry. Up in the murkiness overhead lightning was thrilling intermittently in brilliant, blurred sheets. There was something grand and awful about being in the very home of the storm, brushing shoulders as it were with the elemental forces themselves. Under circumstances of less exigency, to hobnob thus would doubtless be most inspiring, but to our little band, staggering along over the uneven half-crusted snow, weary in limb and battered by chilling blast, it represented the consummation of adversity."

Seeking shelter below Azimuth Ridge in the continuing storm . . .

"Was an absolutely unrelenting fate pursuing us that we should be held up here for the remainder of the night? The rain had now ceased and after all it was rather pleasant to follow the wet rocks munching such morsels of food as ingenuity could extricate from the rucksacks. A thousand feet down, the great white way of Silvertip glacier led alluringly towards camp, apparently but a stone's throw away. Yet we stood about as good a chance of making a safe descent to it over the wet grass, as the proverbial blind man did of succeeding in his search of a dark room for a black cat that was not there.

However, by an extraordinary stroke of good fortune we were spared the need of a trail. Just as the cold was making us distinctly uncomfortable, the clouds parted in the south, and to our joy, we beheld a big yellow moon sailing serenely through a clear sky. There was only a glimpse to be sure, for presently it dodged behind a watery bank of mist, but the effect on us was electrical. That fine warm supper going to waste at camp might be ours after all. Hurriedly gathering up our belongings and adjusting the rope we resumed the way. Although dark bastions of cumulus were drifting across the heavens, constantly widening openings between gave sufficient light to dinstinguish the footing, and before long we were bathed in the unobstructed radiance itself. What a climax to a day already crowded with bewildering surprises! It seemed incredible that these snowy névés now glowing with soft irridescence could be the black frozen deserts of an hour before."

These are the Selkirks - Nelson's Mountains.

EPILOGUE

Over 70 years have elapsed since Howard Palmer's adventures, and yet little has changed in the Selkirks. Only the glaciers have receded, where once they ground their way to much lower elevations among the peaks. Men continue to pit their strength against the strongholds of the Selkirk Mountains with only one advantage over Palmer, that is the ease of approach to the high mountain valleys.

In Palmer's day the Trans-Canada highway through the Roger's Pass did not exist, only the Canadian Pacific Railway provided access to the Selkirks. Near the summit of the pass, the now absent Glacier House was the center of Canadian alpinism. Today Banff has assumed that importance, and the automobile allows climbers to range far and wide.

Still, the Selkirks resist total ease of access. There are only a few logging roads leading toward the heart of the ranges leaving much of the country desolate. Few unclimbed peaks remain, but the land with its wild mountains and high valleys ringed by ice continue to seduce those who enjoy nature.

The spirit of the mountaineer thrives in the Selkirks and though 100 years has gone by since man first explored, the area remains much the same. You will still encounter grizzlies roaming in flower burdened meadows; water tumbling down mountain flanks, then placidly reflecting the surrounding peaks; and wind plastering snow against the crags and shrubs of the high alpine reaches whisking bare the ridges where mountain goats forage through the winter.

The Selkirks are still here and will remain long after this book becomes tattered with age. Hopefully they will be respected by mankind and revered as a part of nature we can always turn to for adventure, knowledge and learning. We need such alternatives in our high pressure world. We need the mountains as we need religion, as we need each other, as we need life.

Return then, to the Selkirks, as I often have. The answers to the questions we seek are out there, in the world of nature - a world we came from, a world we will always return to.

facing page
Autumn Foliage   *R. W. Laurilla*

NOTES

The Selkirks - Nelson's Mountains
[1]Eugene F. Boss, "Place Names in the Purcells", ACC Journal, Vol. 59, 1976, p. 37.

The Bugaboos
[1]A. H. MacCarthy, "The Howser and Bugaboo Spires, Purcell Range", Canadian Alpine Journal, Vol, VIII, p. 26.
[2]Ibid., p. 27.

The Southern Selkirks
[1]Mt. Tupper - named after Sir Charles Tupper, famous Nova Scotia politician and one of the Fathers of Confederation.

[2]Mt. MacDonald - named after Sir John A. MacDonald, Canada's First Prime Minister and Father of Confederation.

[3]W. L. Putnam and R. Kruszyna, "Interior Ranges of B.C. - South", 1972, p.

[4]Bates McKee, "Cascadia", McGraw-Hill, 1972, p. 76.

The Battle Range
[1]Howard Palmer, "Mountaineering and Exploration in the Selkirks", G. P. Putnam's Sons, New York and London, The Knickerbocker Press, 1914, p. 100.

[2]Ibid, p. 100.

Asulkan Pass
[1]William S. Green, "Among the Selkirk Glaciers", MacMillan and Co., London, 1890, p. 127.

[2]Ibid., p. 128.

[3]William Spotswood Green, "Among the Selkirk Glaciers", MacMillan and Co., London, England, 1890.

Clachnacudainn
[1]A. O. Wheeler, "The Selkirk Range", Government Printing Bureau, 1905, p. 40.

Balu Pass
[1]Dan McCowan, "Animals of the Canadian Rockies", 1936, p. 120.

The Major's Mountain
[1]"Appalachia", July, 1897, Vol. VIII, No. III.

facing page
Frost at Isaac Creek　　　　*U. Veideman*

BIBLIOGRAPHY

Dowling, Phil, The Mountaineers, Famous Climbers in Canada, Edmonton: Hurtig, 1979.

Flint, Richard Foster, Glacial and Pleistocene Geology, New York, Wiley & Sons, 1967.

Fraser, Esther, Wheeler, Banff: Summerthought, 1978.

Fraser, Esther, The Canadian Rockies, Early Travels and Explorations, Edmonton: Hurtig, 1969.

Green, William Spotswood, Among the Selkirk Glaciers, London, England: MacMillan and Co.,1890.

Kain, Conrad, Where The Clouds Can Go, edited by J. Monroe Thorington, New York: The American Alpine Club, 1979.

McKee, Bates, Cascadia, The Geologic Evolution of the Pacific Northwest, New York: McGraw-Hill, 1972.

McCowan, Dan, Animals of the Canadian Rockies, New York: Dodd, Mead and Co., 1936.

Palmer, Howard, Mountaineering and Exploration in the Selkirks, New York and London: G.P. Putnam's Sons, Knickerbocker Press, 1914.

Putnam, William L., A Climber's Guide to the Interior Ranges of British Columbia, Springfield, MA: The American Alpine Club and The Alpine Club of Canada, 1975.

Wheeler, A. O., The Selkirk Range, Ottawa: Government Printing Bureau, 1905.

JOURNALS

PERIODICALS

MacCarthy, Albert H., The Howser and Bugaboo Spires, Canadian Alpine Journal, Vol. VIII.

Lake Windermere Valley Echo, Supplement of 1977, Invermere, British Columbia.

overleaf
Alpine Meadows   *R. W. Laurilla*

facing page
Giant Cedars   *R. W. Laurilla*